MW00562954

Sacred Nature

Material Religion in Antiquity (MaReA)

During the last decades, the search for religious materiality has strongly increased among scholars interested in analyzing religious beliefs in both ancient and contemporaneous societies. In particular, since the publication of Renfrew's identification of archaeological correlates of religious practices in 1985, archaeologists have increasingly rectified the epistemological trajectory identified by Hawkes inwhich the reconstruction of ancient forms of religiosity appears as an impossible task for the archaeologists.

Such a material approach to ancient religiosity follows that path traced during the last decades in the field of the anthropology of religion as well as in other fields of religious studies, because an idealist approach to religions that focuses mainly on the 'beliefs' and puts aside the material and practical part of religious beliefs does not have a long life.

Such a material approach to ancient religiosity follows that path traced during the last decades in the field of the anthropology of religion as well as in other fields of religious studies, because an idealist approach to religions that focuses mainly on the 'beliefs' and puts aside the material and practical part of religious beliefs does not have a long life.

Such a 'material turn' it is also necessary in investigating ancient religious practices and beliefs, and, thus, it will be main goal of this series to broadly investigate archaeological contexts in which clear correlates of religious practices and beliefs (e.g., visual, architectural, sensorial, textual) were unearthed. In so doing, the series will publish every year a volume dedicated to a specific topic proposed by either the editor or by one of the members of the scientific committee. In some circumstances and, if the scientific committee will find it fitting with the series objectives, the series volume will represent either an edited volume of conference proceedings or a single authored monograph.

In conclusion, the newly founded series Material Religion in Antiquity (MaReA) aims at becoming a source for scholars and students interested in investigating how to approach the materialization of ancient religious practices and beliefs through case-studies as well as theoretical and methodological approaches.

Sacred Nature

Animism and materiality in ancient religions

edited by

Nicola Laneri and Anna Perdibon

Material Religion in Antiquity (MaReA) Volume 2

OXBOW | books
Oxford & Philadelphia

CAMNES
CENTER FOR ANCIENT MEDITERRANEAN
AND NEAR EASTERN STUDIES

Published in the United Kingdom in 2023 by
OXBOW BOOKS
The Old Music Hall, 106-108 Cowley Road, Oxford, OX4 1JE

and in the United States by
OXBOW BOOKS
1950 Lawrence Road, Havertown, PA 19083

Hardback edition: ISBN 978-1-78925-917-9
Digital Edition: ISBN 978-1-78925-918-6 (ePub)

A CIP record for this book is available from the British Library

Library of Congress Control Number: 2022944327

Printed in the United Kingdom by Short Run Press

For a complete list of Oxbow titles, please contact:

UNITED KINGDOM
Oxbow Books
Telephone (01865) 241249
Email: oxbow@oxbowbooks.com
www.oxbowbooks.com

UNITED STATES OF AMERICA
Oxbow Books
Telephone (610) 853-9131, Fax (610) 853-9146
Email: queries@casemateacademic.com
www.casemateacademic.com/oxbow

Oxbow Books is part of the Casemate Group

Front cover: Illustrated by Karen Abend.
Back cover: Standing stones in intact frame. Chigirtein Nuur, Sagsay sum (photo: Esther Jacobson-Tepfer).

Contents

Contributors

DORALICE FABIANO
Dipartimento di Studi Letterari, Filologici e Linguistici, Università degli Studi di Milano, Via Festa del Perdono 7, 20122, Milan, Italy

GRAHAM HARVEY
Department of Religious Studies, Faculty of Arts and Social Sciences, The Open University, Walton Hall, Milton Keynes, MK7 6AA, UK

ERICA HILL
Department of Social Sciences, University of Alaska Southeast, 11066 Auke Lake Way, Juneau, AK 99801, USA

ESTHER JACOBSON-TEPFER
Department of the History of Art and Architecture, University of Oregon, Eugene, Oregon, USA

MARI JOERSTAD
Vancouver School of Theology, 6015 Walter Gage Rd, Vancouver, BC V6T 1Z1, Canada

NICOLA LANERI
University of Catania and School of Religious Studies, CAMNES, Via Del Giglio 15, 50123 Florence, Italy

VALENTINO NIZZO
Museo Nazionale Etrusco di Villa Giulia, Piazzale di Villa Giulia 9, 00196, Rome, Italy

ANNA PERDIBON
School of Religious Studies, CAMNES, Via Del Giglio 15, 50123 Florence, Italy

SETH RICHARSON
Oriental Institute 312, The University of Chicago, 1155 East 58th Street, Chicago, IL 60637, USA

Introduction. Sacred nature: animism and materiality in ancient religions

Anna Perdibon and Nicola Laneri

Both humans and the animals and plants on which they depend for a livelihood must be regarded as fellow participants in the same world, a world that is at once social and natural. (Ingold 2000, 87)

Sacred nature?

The very notions of nature, culture and even religion are critical and currently being called into question from a variety of perspectives, including in light of the ecological crisis we are living in, generating a plentiful supply of studies, approaches and discussions. These blossoming fields – often regarded as religion and ecology, religion, nature and culture, or religion and the environment – delve into exploring various human–environmental relationships. Particular attention is given to calling into question the nature/culture dichotomy with other divides – such as subject/object, spirit/body, immanent/transcendent, spiritual/material, *etc* – that developed within the Euro-Western cultural framework. As argued by Sahlins, 'the determination of nature as pure materiality – absent gods, incarnate spirits, or any such non-human persons– is a unique Western invention' (Sahlins 2000, 564). Such a concept of nature as a mere object for exploration and resource to exploit, deprived of any sacredness and divinity, and in stark opposition to the domain of humans (*i.e.* culture), was also unknown within the Western European context, at least until after the Middle Ages and the Renaissance. Accordingly, this dichotomy should be considered an abstract piece of Western intellectualism developed through the centuries in scholarly circles: a notion alien to ancient, pre-Modern, non-Western and non-hegemonic cultures, cosmologies and spiritualities. Thus, exploring non-Modern and non-Western religious beliefs, experiences and practices through the history of humans on the planet seems vital in order to highlight the plurality of ontologies, cosmologies, epistemologies within the shared history of humans on the planet (Feldt 2016; Joerstad 2019; Perdibon 2019; Graham 2021).

Sacred Nature is diving into questions such as: how did the ancient communities conceive, engage and represent phenomena and beings that we call Nature? How are the cosmos, landscape and environment expressed in ancient religious expressions, practices, beliefs, narratives and representations? How did deities, spirits, trees, the land, water, animals, stones and objects relate to one another and participate to human religious and spiritual experiences? What relationships generated from the myriad encounters of specific natures with cultures? And which cosmovisions? What would a sacred nature mean and be engaged with? How can we reconstruct vividly and interpret correctly ancient religions and cultures, understand their ways to live and know the world through the traces left by written, iconographical and material sources?

In the attempt to try reply to some of these interconnected questions, the theories and approaches drawn from religious studies, anthropology and ethnography are precious pathways to challenge and even overcome our conceptual framewroks, as ways to enhance new outlooks and interpretations on the multiplicity of relationships human communities had with their local environments. This volume, offspring from the international online workshop *Sacred Nature: Animism and Materiality in Ancient Religions* (Florence, Italy, 20–21 May 2021), aims at stirring up a starkly inter-disciplinary and religious-anthropological discussion about the diverse conceptions, representations, practices and engagements toward what we call Nature in ancient religious cultures of the Old and New World. In particular, we reflect on animism as a fruitful analytical term and bring it into dialogue with the discussions and approaches of the material turn for shedding new light onto the ways ancient cultures represented, engaged and understood their encompassing landscapes with their other-than-human inhabitants.

Old and new animism

Introduced by Edward Tylor in his book *Primitive Cultures* (1871), the traditional term 'animism' refers to the belief that non-human beings possess a life and a spiritual essence. However, due to its colonialist and evolutionistic connotations, the classical, old usage of this term has been progressively dismissed. Until recently, when scholars of religion and anthropology have recovered it in a new, relational and decolonizing way (Hallowell 1960; Bird-David 1999; Bird Rose 1999; Ingold 2000; Descola 2005; 2013; Harvey 2013a; 2013b; 2017; Sahlins 2018). At its core lies an encompassing notion of personhood that is inclusive of the non-humans. According to Graham Harvey, 'animists recognise that the world is full of persons, only some of whom are human, and that life is always lived in relationship with others. Animism is lived out in various ways that are all about learning to act respectfully (carefully and constructively) towards and among other persons' (Harvey 2017, xiii). With personhood being acknowledged in spirits, deities, animals, plants, stones, mountains, seas, rivers, places and human artefacts alike, nature is acknowledged and experienced as a living and animate community, place of agency, relationality and spirituality.

The new animist understanding of personhood and relationality challenges the dualities informing Modernity such as nature/culture, object/subject, immanent/transcendent, material/spiritual, body/soul. New animism is increasingly becoming a research field and analytical concept that researches and dialogues with relational, embodied and material approaches, ideas, representations and practices in which humans engage with other natural elements, animals, and things. As such it contains immense potential for generating wider discussions in the study of ancient and contemporary religions.

Materiality

New animism converges in several ways with the thriving research field of material religion. This new field, often regarded as 'material turn', is gaining ground in the study of religions and promotes the idea that religion can be better understood and defined through considering the matrix of relations between knowledge, experience, beliefs, practices, places, things (Morgan 2021). Approaching the study of religions with a material perspective means asking: 'how does religion happens materially?'. This question translates in approaching religion by starting 'with the assumption that things, their use, their valuation, and their appeal are not something added to a religion, but rather inextricable from it' (Meyer *et al.* 2010, 209). Accordingly, religion is done and co-created by a complex and dynamic network of agents, be they bodies, rituals, places, objects, images, stones, rivers, seas, trees, sounds, tastes, smells, as much as by texts, minds, beliefs, spirits. In this line, any religious belief is a reticulation of relationships among actors, where each aspect of this network of actors enjoys an element of agency (Latour 2005), while practices are defined as 'ways of activating bodies, things, and places, recognizing in their interrelations a presence or voice or power that engages humans and their institutions and communities' (Meyer *et al.* 2010, 209). Religion is thus approached and addressed as an every-day, sensuous and embodied practice that enhances people to establish, maintain and re-enact different relations with the local other-than-human community within a deeply relational cosmos.

Nature as a relational community of other-than-human beings: the contributions

Sacred Nature collects and brings into conversation the researches and perspectives of scholars of different disciplines (archaeology, anthropology, art, philology, studies of religions). Experts of different geographical areas and historical periods, the contributors discuss and shed new light onto emic notions of religion, sacredness, personhood, nature, agency, communication, community, justice and care in ancient religions of the Old and New World. After an introducing theoretical chapter on nature, sacredness and animism, the authors bring us into a journey starting from the West Arctic America and Mongolia, through the ancient Near East, Greece and Italian peninsula, to the Biblical world projecting into present times. What we hope is that this dialoguing book will be just a starting point for further dialogues and researches into an increasingly relevant field.

Drawing from his definition of animists and animism and its applicability to ancient peoples, what Harvey seeks to do in Chapter 1 is to demonstrate how the discussions about 'Modern and animist ways of making and relating in the world *might* lead to better or fuller understandings of the possible ancient worlds'. Harvey advances a 'cross-cultural, trans-temporal pluriversal experiment', undertaking a journey into the meaning of 'sacred nature' in Modern and animist ontologies, as an invitation to reflect on what '"sacred nature" *could have meant* in ancient worlds'.

Immersing into the story of the Nature/Culture dichotomy, Harvey digs into the differences and pluralities of human–environmental relationships in both Modernity and animism. While stressing that there is no single Modernity nor single animist cultural complex, he shows how Modernists and animists do not see mountains, stones, animals and plants differently, but rather one sees Nature where the others see 'communities of kin'. Animist world(view)s as strongly relational, plural in their dynamic interactions and engagements with the immediate landscape, with some relations closer than others, and where some places, beings and objects can be approached as sacred. Thus, animism(s) is here utilized as 'main example of an other-than-Modern world-making in which the term "Nature" would be dissonant and distracting'.

Pausing on the key themes of new animism – such as belief, sacrality, nature, culture, taboo and the much debated term of other-than-human person, Harvey invites us to engage with relationality and materiality in research and teaching about religious cultures past and present. By reclaiming relationality as a key term for animist world-making, Harvey pinpoints the vitality of dialoguing among historical and contemporary religious cultures in order to explore different ways of 'living and cooperating' with(in) the larger-than-human world of ancient communities.

Exploring watercrafts of western Arctic coasts through ethnohistorical and ethnographic sources, Erica Hill uncovers some aspects of a complex relational network that linked humans, marine mammals, plants, sea and 'objects'. Chapter Two deals with rich network of material, social and symbolic relations around the construction, maintenance and usage of two forms of skin-covered watercraft – the *umiaq*, a large open boat, and the smaller, decked *qayaq* (or kayak). In Inupiat and Yupiit societies, the dependence on sea animals and their hunting was almost complete: animals were understood and approached as persons according to strict protocols of conduct. Whaling, in particular, was a highly sophisticated form of hunting among the Bering Sea coastal inhabitants.

In this hunting complex system and etiquette, Hill argues that the *umiaq* was a symbolically powerful and hybrid assemblage and 'object-being', which acted as active mediator between men and women and among humans, plants and animals. She begins by presenting the process of construction of the *umiaq* from drifwood (primarily spruce) and bearded seals' or walrus' skin, with an overview on the gendered social roles and values involved. According to Hill, 'the *umiaq* was the product of multiple transformational processes that connected men, women, plants and animals. These processes were relational, based upon the cooperative labor of husbands and wives, extended families and kin groups'.

Such processes inform the creation of assemblages, where the social and the material are pulled together forming new constellations of human, plant and animal bodies that function in ways distinct from their component parts. As hybrid assemblage, the *umiaq* emerges as a composite artefact, that 'defies attempts to separate living from non-living, land and sea, nature and culture'. At the same time, the *umiaq* acted as an agent itself, an animated 'object-being' mediating relations between human and animal communities. By exploring stories, practices and rituals involving the *umiaq*, Hill highlights the *umiaq* of as an 'object-being', provided with an (even aesthetic) agency, mediating and connecting humans and whales within the complex world of land, ice and water.

Animism is explored through the cutting-edge notion of liminality in Chapter Three. Esther Jacobson-Tefter take us into a journey into signs of liminality in ancient Altai stone monuments, by reading a '*de facto* pictorial text' comprised by the rock art and surface structures that trace back human life in the high valleys. In her understanding of animism, the concept of liminality is expanded from the rites of passage 'to include the substances or forms of being through which those rites carry us'. Analyzing the compositions and motifs of birthing or guardian women, hunting scenes, chariots, horses and great birds, Jacobson-Tepefer offers a vivid portrayal of a world constantly engaging with life and death.

This petroglyphic material reveals the belief systems of Altai people in the late Bronze Age, according to which when a life is taken (*e.g.*, while hunting), it must be replenished. The figure embodying such reciprocity is the birthing woman, who acts also as the guardian of the roads that lead to the land of the dead. The female image overlaps with that of the spirit of the mountain, both protector and generator of game, but also the realm of the dead. With her, horses, with or without chariots, were understood as the means by which the dead made that last journey. The presence of birds hints at the notion of rebirth thanks to their agency in allowing the dead to reincarnate. At the same time, the animals and hunting scenes re-affirm the human dependency on the more-than-human world. The Altai rock art speaks of a way of thinking and being in the world where the boundaries between human and non-human, living and dead, are porous and impermanent, and that this dynamic balance had to be appropriately taken care of.

The ways of knowing and relating with the non-urban landscape through divination in ancient Mesopotamia is the subject of Chapter Four. Seth Richardson offers a survey on Babylonian divinatory practices of the Late Old Babylonian period (ca. 17th century BCE) to analyze the epistemic discourse of divination concerning human movements through non-urban spaces. The (mainly sheep) liver divination was widely practised throughout the centuries in the ancient Near Eastern cultures and, in the surveyed period, it was utilized to predict and inquire about travelling conditions across the open territory while moving between cities, temples, forts and camps. The catalogues of omens that form part of the administrative texts reveal both how deeply ingrained was divination within the administrative praxis and provide insights into the perception of the outer territory as a hostile and dangerous, difficult to surveille and move through.

Richardon explores the omens literature and praxis concerning journeys and expeditions of soldiers from fortresses and camps to cities, uncovering aspects of divination as a craft and insights into the political and economic history of Middle Bronze Age in Mesopotamia. In doing this, he turns his attention to the role of the landscape itself and the relationship between divination and geography. A 'particular homology between divination and landscape' emerges, where the liver is a map of landscape, a microcosm mirroring the macrocosm of a potentially hostile and always unpredictable landscape. This understanding is corroborated by the terms utilized for both reading the liver and the territory. Such cartographic system can be understood as a form of 'sacred nature': a relational cosmos in which people, land, animals and divinity were communicating and bound up in an analogical system of reference. In this picture, a relevant detail is highlighted: the praxis of divination was more concerned with knowing and engaging with an unknown territory in the present, rather than with predicting the future.

Taking on the classical animist understanding of the tree nymphs in the Greek religion, Doralice Fabiano offers a new interpretation on the relationships between trees and nymphs in Chapter 5. Exploring a passage of the *Homeric hymn to Aphrodite* (vv. 256–272), which is the most comprehensive description of nymphs in archaic Greek literature, Fabiano calls into question the traditional interpretation of nymphs as 'tree spirits'. In the literary passage examined, the life of the nymphs appears to be blurring the borders of life and death and strictly entangled with that of the trees. Not matching human or divine existence, the nymphs, despite not ageing, are born and die. In the same way and time that the nymphs come to life and die, trees sprout and dry out. Moreover, the text reports that such trees, like firs and oaks, are called sacred places, and a particular honour given to them: a respect that is manifested and embodied in the prohibition to cut or damage the arboreal beings.

Fabiano explores the several similarities and connections between nymphs and trees, addressing their consubstantiality, physical representation, other-than-human ageing and locality. Moreover, she considers the roles of trees in the ritual contexts by focusing on two archaeological sites in Greece. Both sacred cave sites, that of Var in Attica and Pharsalus in Thessaly, disclose direct evidence of a lively nymphs' cult. In the inscriptions found *in situ*, vegetation emerges as playing an important role in both engaging with and 'representing the goddesses' – especially concerning the devotional life of men possessed by the nymphs (*nympholepts*) who grew gardens in those spaces.

Thinking through the theoretical framework of the cognitive study of religions, Fabiano argues that trees are not nymphs' bodies, according to the dichotomous framework of opposition between spiritual and material, soul and body. Rather, as shown in the explored textual and ritual contexts, 'trees can be considered as a sensible "double" of the nymphs, that is a material object making nymphs visible to mortals'. At the same time, such association of trees and nymphs in nymphs' cult expressed through gardening should be seen as a way to cultivate relationships with gods. According to this understanding, taking care of plants seems correspond to the '"care" humans owe to divinities', with the action of planting reflecting 'the fact that nymphs as local deities are thought to "root" individuals in a specific territory'.

The social life of images and objects though their histories and contexts in peninsular Italy is examined in Chapter Six. Drawing from the notion of objects as agents with their own history and changes in meanings and roles, and ability to interact with different contexts, Valentino Nizzo offers a survey of jewels crafted and founded in the Italian peninsula and dated from the 8th–6th centuries BCE, outlining the dynamics of contact and assimilation between indigenous craftsmen of the Italian world and Eastern and Greek immigrants to the peninsula.

Nizzo follows the changes and hybridization of the bird and solar boat motifs with those portraying the anthropomorphic figure of the *Potnia theron* 'Lady of the animals' and the *Despotes hippon*, 'lord of the horses'. Through a careful survey of the iconographic motifs in different areas of the peninsula, Nizzo traces a series of cultural processes that move in parallel and almost simultaneously. Stressing that 'the perception of meaning can change according to the "social life" of the objects to which the image is associated and their various possible destinations', he points out that during the 7th century BCE, the indigenous Italian motif of the solar boat, often accompanied by a bird motif, progressively lost its original meaning and function. This occurred due to a process of assimilation of Near Eastern and Greek mythical and iconographical repertoire, including that of the hybrid figure of the *Potnia theron*.

Chapter Seven explores the roles and responsibilities of the land and its other other-than-human inhabitants in the Biblical world. Drawing from the theoretical framework of new animism, Mari Joerstad delves into texts as Genesis 1 and Leviticus 18–26, in order to uncover how the ancient authors of the Hebrew Bible conceptualized divine responsibilities and the notion of justice inclusive of the other-than-humans. Starting by assuming Harvey's definition of animists as an accurate description of ancient Israelites, Joerstad argues that other-than-human creatures actively participated in the divine cosmos. She delves into the concepts of righteousness, obedience and disobedience by considering texts where plants, trees, water, animals and the land itself receive divinely appointed responsibilities, including those cases in which the other-than-human persons fail, or are disobedient to accomplish them. The consequences of any such disobedience are interpreted as sickness, grief and sin. The texts analyzed suggest that Biblical authors saw no sharp distinction between human and other-than-human responsibilities. In this line, 'every creature depends on every other creature to fulfil their obligations. When one creature fails, everyone suffers'.

At the core of this portrayal of the Biblical ontology lies the notion that all creatures have the encompassing responsibility to sustain and perpetuate life. Indeed, Joerstad focuses on the ways in which each creature contributes and is interconnected to the others for making communal health possible, where humans are one of the many actors involved. Accordingly, community emerges as fully broader-than-human, where plants, animals, humans, minerals, land and water are all participating in a shared and reciprocal cosmos, seeking to maintain and restore righteousness. This final chapter not only offers a fascinating understanding of the Biblical worldview as practically ecological or deeply relational, but also questions what this interpretation of the Bible might mean in restoring environmental justice in current times.

Attempting to recover from the midst of the past and explore the ways in which humans engaged with the more-than-human world, is more than a scholarly exercise of research and interpretation. It is relevant for enabling us to image and draw inspiration from the past through myths, stories, rituals, objects that speak of a profound inter-connection among beings and places of the cosmos, of protocols for establishing and maintaining relationships with the wholeness of life. What emerges in this rich volume is a multi-layered and multi-dimensional portrayal of different specific relationships between humans and their surrounding world in ancient times. Goddesses, trees and nymphs, whales and watercrafts, water and ice, livers and objects, land and mountains, deers and birds, women and men all partook to a relational cosmos perceived as a broader-than-human community, where every being had a role, and humans' duty is to learn and know how to engage appropriately and respectfully with each other-than-human person and the dimensions of life. What we hope to have achieved in this book is to define 'sacred nature' as a relational model in which the other-than-human beings are inextricably involved with humans in constructing modern and ancient cosmologies.

References

Bird-David, N. (1999) 'Animism' revisited: personhood, environment, and relational epistemology. *Current Anthropology* 40 (S1), 67–91.
Bird Rose, D. (1999) Indigenous ecologies and an ethic of connection. In N. Low (ed.) *Global Ethics and Environment*, 175–187. London, Taylor & Francis.
Descola, P. (2005) *Beyond Nature and Culture.* Chicago IL, University of Chicago Press.
Descola, P. (2013) Beyond nature and culture. In Harvey (ed) 2013a, 77–91.
Feldt, L. (2016) Religion, nature, and ambiguous space in ancient Mesopotamia: The mountain wilderness in Old Babylonian religious narratives. *Numen* 63, 347–382.

Graham, E.-J. (2021) *Reassembling Religion in Roman Italy*. London, Routledge.

Hallowell, A.I. (1960) Ojibwa ontology, behavior, and world view. In S. Diamond (ed.) *Culture in History*, 19–52. New York, Columbia University Press.

Harvey, G. (2013a) *Handbook of Contemporary Animism*. Durham, Acumen.

Harvey, G. (2013b) *Food, Sex and Strangers. Understanding Religion as Everyday Life*. Durham, Acumen.

Harvey, G. (2017) *Animism: respecting the living world*. London, Hurst.

Ingold, T. (2000) *The Perception of the Environment. Essays on livelihood, dwelling and skill*. London/New York, Routledge.

Joerstad, M. (2019) *The Hebrew Bible and Environmental Ethics*. Cambridge, Cambridge University Press.

Latour, B. (1993) *We Have Never Been Modern*. New York, Harvester Wheatsheaf.

Latour, B. (2005), *Reassembling the Social: an introduction to actor-network-theory*. Oxford, Oxford University Press.

Meyer, B., Morgan, D., Paine C. and Plate, S.B. (2010) The origin and mission of Material Religion. *Religion* 40, 207–211.

Morgan, D. (2021) *The thing about religion: an introduction to the material study of religions*. The Chapel Hill, University of North Carolina Press.

Perdibon, A. (2019) *Mountains and Trees, Rivers and Springs. Animistic Beliefs and Practices in Ancient Mesopotamian Religion*. Wiesbaden, Harrassowitz.

Sahlins, M. (2018) On the ontological scheme of Beyond Nature and Culture. In M. Astor-Aguilera and G. Harvey (eds) *Rethinking Relations and Animism: personhood and materiality*, 15–24, London/New York, Routledge.

Sahlins, M. (2000) *Culture in Practice: selected essays*. New York, Zone Books.

Tylor, E.B. (2000) *Primitive Culture: researches into the development of mythology, philosophy, religion, art and culture*. London, John Murray

Chapter 1

Before Nature: perspectives from new animist world-making

Graham Harvey

Many contemporary Indigenous people treat the world as a series of communities of living persons, most of whom are not human. They encourage and inculcate life-long improvements in respectfully interacting with their relations – human or otherwise. Some relations are only closer than others and may involve interactions which could be considered 'sacred'. That is, locally valued forms of respectful etiquette typically inform sacred ceremonies that make, remake or maintain the world. In recent multidisciplinary debates inspired by new-found respect for Indigenous knowledges, these and similar themes have influenced the ontological turn, the new animism and Actor-Network Theory. My purpose is not to assert that ancient religionists must be interpreted according to animist protocols. Rather, it is to provoke further questioning of the application of Modernity's nature/culture dualism to the other-than-Modern religions of the ancient world.

In a moment, I will offer a story. This frees me and you from the tyranny of the 'God-trick' of imagining we can gain an objective position from which to fully comprehend and completely encompass unassailable facts (Haraway 1988). It frees us to explore truths about the (plural) worlds we live in, among and through (King 2003; Gibson *et al.* 2015, ii). It allows us to be pedestrian: walking slowly, noticing the here-and-now, saying what comes to us, rather than rising above the messy flows so as to theorize dispassionately a universal reality. Story-telling does not *describe* reality but *produces* possibilities through which we and others move with more-or-less ease or restraint. I happily imagine that colleagues familiar with ancient deities may be less likely to stumble onto the pedestal of that monotheistic-influenced scholarly 'God-trick'. At the conclusion of this article I will reference one of those other-than-monotheistic deities: the increasingly irritable Gaia who now poses difficult and urgent questions (Stengers 2015), some perhaps propelled by doubts that we are serious about sacred nature.

One story *requires* the telling of second and third and subsequent stories – amplifying or contesting the first. The point of the opening story and of the whole article is to experiment further with what Isabelle Stengers calls 'manners of living and cooperating' with(in) the larger-than-human world, despite some of them having been 'destroyed in the name of progress' (Stengers 2015, 12). I gratefully acknowledge that I am following a path well-trodden by many Indigenous hosts. It is a path which remains open and could bear more travellers into the 'world in which many worlds are possible' (Marcos 1996, section iii; Escobar 2020). By saying some things about Modernities and animisms, and especially about their (re)making and (re)storying of the world(s), I hope to enable further conversations about 'sacred nature' in ancient religions and cultures. My capitalisation of words like 'Modern' and 'Nature' is intended to direct attention to the world-making (and un-making) of particular cultural projects – it will undoubtedly provoke objection and I hope, more discussion. That is, such capitals shout out that these are not neutral (natural?) descriptive terms but signs of particular world-making missions.

Having said that, I also acknowledge that my story and my article will also be in need of further conversations with colleagues who have a better grasp of ancient literatures and materialities. My contribution is an effort to understand what the collocation of 'sacred' and 'nature' can achieve within resistance to the Modern monofication of the worlds (Savransky 2021, 11). It might, for example, tell us something different about ancient and contemporary worlds that could be missed *if* Modernity's separatist and extractivist ontology is allowed to continue claiming precedence as the best interpretative lens.

Here, then, is the story of then, now, there and again: Before we were introduced to Nature we lived in a world of varied relations with all existences. We were always among kin. No being or thing was not kin to others. Encountering differences provided occasions for conversations that composed new relations. But before we had learnt all the local rules of etiquette for engaging respectfully with each, let alone all, of those we encountered in the larger-than-human community, 'Nature' interrupted. We were instructed in how to reduce our kin group. We were rewarded for distancing ourselves from the vibrantly living, loudly communicative, relational world we had lived in. 'Objects' – inert materialities – were introduced to us. Explicit didacticism and seductive enculturation shaped us to live in a new world. A world in which humans are distinctive and are expected to increase efforts to be separate from 'Nature'. A world in which 'Culture' enchanted us (but we were led to see it as rational choice not as enchantment) with its kaleidoscopic but always human forms: arts, economy, leisure, politics, religion, sports, cuisine, pet-ownership and more. We learnt to believe in belief as an explanation for the strange relations people in 'other cultures' have with the(ir) worlds but were encouraged to be tolerant while they made/joined progress. In schools and universities an audacious sleight of hand and mind and language tricked us into thinking of knowledge as parcelled out into silos labelled Social and Natural Sciences, and then further subdivided and disciplined. We came to accept that the world is similarly parcelled out, and to participate in the disciplining of reality, the reduction of relations. Ironically, we have specialized in not seeing things that escape the subject matter allocated by our disciplining at the same time as we imagine ourselves having the objectivity necessary to propose universal truths. We have come to assume that the majority of the world is not social but silent, not relatives but resource. We have colluded in our own extraction from the kinship-world, and we have therefore benefited (or so we have learnt to think) by being able to extract all we wish from that resource-world. We were kin, now we are Modern.

This is a story that could be about different 'we'. It could be about 'we' people-alive-today who were once children but were grown up into Moderns (Latour 1993). As this 'we' we talked with tables and toys as well as with parents, siblings and companionable animals. The story could be about 'we' people-with-a-history shaped by the Nature/Culture separation who were once not-Modern. As Modernity has taken ground globally, almost all children in the world today are subject to learning to see Nature – out there, away from us humans, waiting (metaphorically, impersonally, impassively and inactively) to be visited when we seek to benefit from recreation or resource-extraction. A few children are still brought up in what might, for now, for ease of communication among we (wholly or partially) Moderns, be considered kinship cultures or gift economies. But as those children grow they will need to know that their kinship worlds are fragile remnants impacted by a Modernity that extracts humans from the(ir) worlds while extracting consumable objects from their relations. Some people will capitulate to the currently dominant Culture and thereby learn to recognize Nature. Some will join resistance groups – learning the etiquette of the larger-than-human world(s) as well as the rules (explicit or subtle) of the all-consuming Modern human-separatist movement. Survival may depend on such biculturalism – as it has and does in other colonising situations.

Clearly my 'once up a time, and now' story is a myth (a word burdened with sloshy bowls of conflicting flavours). Like all good myths it conveys truths. It is not false. But it is a story. It is not the whole truth but a provocation of thinking and an invitation to reflect, riff, revise and re-tell – never using all the same words and therefore always involved in worlds-being-made. There is, for instance, no single Modernity. There is no single not-Modernity. There is no single path of childhood development. There is no straight path of cultural development. There is only the pluriverse in which worlds of scintillating difference are necessarily braided or tangled together, sometimes harmoniously, sometimes ruinously (de la Cadena and Blaser 2018; Escobar 2020; Savransky 2021). Modernity's 'others' are not the past of Modernity – nor are they necessarily in the process of becoming the past. But such others are all too often ideologically and imaginatively theorized (by Modernists and postmodernists) as

> excluded from participation in the construction of a world in common by being rendered part of a past in the process of being overcome by mechanisms of modernity initiated independently of that participation (Bhambra 2007, 55).

The actual and possible worlds (not excluding Modernity) co-compose the current moment – as they have always done.

In short, the first story is flawed – or perhaps facetted. Nonetheless, Modernity's education is powerful and most of 'we' have been shaped to assume that there is a place called Nature and another called Culture. We have learnt that humans are separate and *should* only treat some existences as kin. We have (mis)heard and (mis)told other world-making stories – ancient and contemporary – in ways that fit the split Nature/Culture worlding of the one-world world (Law 2004, 7; also see 1994; 2015; 2019).

The story continues in heroic mode: We can resist, many do resist. But it is never easy. It is certainly not as easy as some academics think. Anyone who suggests that Modernity's Nature reification and its particular Nature/Culture distinction are globally dominant, as I do here, will be told to read proliferating journal articles and monographs that demonstrate the diversity of contemporary cultures or modernities in which 'nature' might label diverse (sometimes agential) realities. But, I object, such articles have not yet changed Modernity. The word 'Nature' still means a realm separate from Culture, a place distinct from humanity (in the same way that theatre stages are distinct from actors, *i.e.*, only as constructed by Modernity [because, of course, stages co-enact the play too]). Just watch any documentary about plants or animals – or about those communities we call lakes, forests, mountains or reefs. You will hear about Nature. Ruled by instinct, lacking full intentionality, programmed to act but not participating as agents, having some (mechanical?) memory but no creative intelligence. Humans will be separated, filtered out. You will only see them if there is a closing 'making of' piece featuring the camera crew or local guides. Or perhaps there will be exoticized 'native' people, adding to the colour because they 'live close to Nature'. Even many Pagan 'nature religionists' (who might be expected to celebrate a vibrant larger-than-human community) tout the benefits of spending time 'in Nature' away from other humans. The greatest adepts among them can stroll through landscapes changed by centuries of human, botanical, animal, climatic and other interactive histories and still imagine themselves in pristine, a-historical, un-human wild places.

In these and other ways, Modernity's human separatists – and those seduced or colonised by this ideology – have not been significantly impacted by any of the critical literature. The foundations and border defences of this Modern world are in little danger of collapsing and can easily be re-pointed or re-plastered by the judicious re-use of the word 'Nature'. We have been acculturated to inhabit this world, this one-world reality. We are naturalized citizens of that world – and this disciplines the ways we understand and re-present 'other cultures' (historical or contemporary) as well as our own never-fully-Modernized world.

Nonetheless, again, to emphasize, it is true that the opening story does not make it sufficiently clear that there is no single entity that is either Modernity or not-Modernity. There are multiple Modernities. There are multiple other-than-modernities. Some of the (only temporally not logically) pre-modern other-than-Modern worlds were also conflicted about the relations of humans with the larger-than-human world. Being kin and being consumers were and are neither the only available options nor necessarily dichotomous opposites. Everybody has to eat somebody. Thus, kin and consumer are labels for some of the possible ways of moving through all of the worlds. In many other-than-Modern cultures, children, foreign visitors and recalcitrant philosophers were and are taught locally appropriate ways of engaging with that world. The necessity of teaching about or acculturation into how to engage with the world (*i.e.*, the fact that it does not 'come naturally') is indicative of the diversity of relations in those and all realities. This might be a key justification for seeking clarity about ancient 'sacred nature'. While gaining a better understanding of ancient worlds we might also pick up more questions to ask of current worlds or for future worlds.

Having said all this, it is also true that just as there is no single Modernity neither is there a single animist cultural complex. This is important because I plan to use animism(s) as my main example of an other-than-Modern world-making in which the term 'Nature' would be dissonant and distracting. Because animisms are strongly relational they are *definitively* plural and diverse. That is, each local animism emphasizes *some* relations more than others. There are close kin (who are not only or always human) and more-or-less distant others, but *these* distances and differences do not (unless infected/inflected by Modernity) generate stories in which 'Nature' conveys any useful, actionable knowledge.

Previously I have encapsulated animism by saying that 'Animists are people who recognize that the world is full of persons, only some of whom are human, and that life is always lived in relationship with others' (Harvey 2017, xiii). It is possible that ancient peoples shared this understanding of the world – a point I shall return to later. However, that is not my primary contention in this article. Rather, I propose that broad sketches of Modern and animist ways of making and relating in the world *might* lead to better or fuller understandings of the possible ancient worlds. In particular, the Modern 'provenance of the notion religion = belief' (Orsi 2015, 19) and the animist notion that stones are worthy of respectful interaction (see below) invite reflection on what 'sacred nature' *could have meant* in ancient worlds. Before advancing this cross-cultural, trans-temporal pluriversal experiment, a revision of my previous encapsulation of animism will also provide an introduction to key themes in new animism debates.

The term 'persons' has worried colleagues and others who have found it either too anthropocentric or too philosophical. My intention was quite different. Inspired by what (North American) Anishinaabeg hosts taught him, Irving Hallowell made good, provocative use of the phrase 'other-than-human persons' to convey a sense of a world in which personhood is not synonymous with 'humans' or 'humanity' (Hallowell 1960).

Had he or, later, I been addressing bears, eagles or stones, we might have written about other-than-bear, other-than-eagle or other-than-stone persons. Why we would address bears, eagles or stones in English is a subject best left to another story. But Anishinaabeg do not need these convoluted, clumsy phrases. Among them, that which is inherent in 'person' is already conveyed in the words for 'human', 'bear', 'eagle' and 'stones'. The grammatical animacy of words like these in Anishinaabe language – and that of neighbouring Indigenous nations – is indicative of vibrant relationships with other-than-human kin in the pervasively animate world (also see Kimmerer 2013; 2015). It is this that led me to write about 'persons'.

The challenge 'other-than-human persons' offers to human-separatist/human-exceptionalist assumptions and assertions is also powerful. The phrase can powerfully interrupt conversations rooted in such worlds. But it does not always lead to recognition or even celebration of other possible worlds in which bears or eagles, stones or stars might add their news and views. It can be an impenetrable barrier. So, I honour the wisdom of preferring to use words like 'relatives' and 'kin' instead (see, for instance, Hogan 2013; Kimmerer 2013; 2015; Haraway 2015; Bird-David 2018). Such kinship terms continue to contest provocatively the notion that humans stand at the pinnacle of evolution and at the centre of the circle of life (as if such fantasy locations really exist). But they are also seductive and inductive, inviting us to realise our relations within the larger-than-human community – one in which we are surrounded by agential and communicative beings rather than by inert and even inept matter.

In addition to the problems caused by the word 'persons', my encapsulation of animism was not intended to suggest that all animists agree on precisely how kinship relationships could or should be enacted. Indeed, it was meant to open up further discussion of the varied locally appropriate etiquettes and rituals of relationship among different animist communities. It was not a statement about categories but about conversations, not an assertion of an idea but an insistence on immediacy, *i.e.*, the actual living of relationships (Naveh and Bird-David 2013). Much of this was already expressed in Hallowell's work. There is, for instance, the frequently cited conversation between Hallowell and an Anishinaabe elder and medicine man, Kiiwiich/Alec Keeper. Hallowell wrote,

> Since stones are grammatically animate, I once asked an old man: Are *all* the stones we see about us here alive? He reflected a long while and then replied, 'No! But *some* are'. (Hallowell 1960, 20; also see Matthews and Roulette 2018)

(Note that 'old man' here is deployed as an honorific, synonymous with 'elder' or 'wise person'.) Again, this might appear to be a conversation about language but it is rich in its social, ecological, political and cosmic implications. As Hallowell goes on to note: 'This qualified answer made a lasting impression on me'. It established his understanding that in conversations with animist Indigenous hosts, 'We are confronted with the philosophical implications of their thought, the nature of the world of being as they conceive it'. The 'world as they conceive it' is also the world that they compose as they interact, seeking to be carefully and constructively respectful of kin, companions and all existences. It is not a world in which it is sensible to ask 'are stones alive?' That is a Modernist question about categories and taxonomies. But, note, Hallowell asked 'are all the stones we see *about us here* alive?' (if you will allow me to change the written emphasis). That is, Hallowell asked Kiiwiich about nearby stones, ones in whose presence their conversation took (made) place. His phrasing was open to the relationality that became the subject of the discussion developing from Kiiwiich's otherwise enigmatic answer.

The elder's answer required more words about stories, rites, greeting etiquette and gift exchange to reveal that his world was one in which knowledge about stones involved those stones. Put differently, Kiiwiich's 'no' answered the Modern obsession with categories while his 'some are' insisted that co-presence and knowledge obligate 'persons' – kin or potential kin – to engage respectfully together. 'No' rejects the Modern question, 'is it alive or dead, animate or inanimate, agential or inert?' '*Some are*' requires different pronouns indicative of assumed liveliness and potential gift-exchange. Because such pronouns are absent from English grammar, we could adopt and extend Marge Piercy's (1979) gender-inclusive pronoun 'per' (from person) or deploy Robin Kimmerer's (2015) 'ki(n)' (singular and plural). At any rate, life and relations, in this kinship world, are more than taxonomic facts or something owned by only some existences. They are interactive engagements, composing beings as they 'become' together. Abbreviating one strand of Elizabeth Povinelli's (2016) 'geontologies' requiem, I might sum this conversation about the animacy (*i.e.*, relationality not ensouled liveliness) of stones by asserting that both biology and geology are necessarily symbiotic and always emergent processes. Neither are 'Nature', both label *some* members of kinship worlds.

Similar arguments have inspired many scholars concerned with the 'new animist', 'new materialist', 'ontological turn' and related scholarly projects to lose interest in locating or theorising souls, spirits, agency or (Cartesian discarnate) minds – among other magical, metaphysical additions to existence. As Tim Ingold says,

> Animacy, then, is not a property of persons imaginatively projected onto the things with which they perceive themselves to be surrounded. Rather ... it is the dynamic, transformative potential of the entire field of relations within which beings of all kinds ... continually and reciprocally bring one another into existence. The animacy of the lifeworld, in short, is not the result of an infusion of spirit into substance, or of agency into materiality, but is rather ontologically prior to their differentiation. (Ingold 2006, 10; also see Merleau-Ponty 1962; Abram 1996; Descola 2014).

All of this leads me to propose revising my earlier encapsulation of animism. Perhaps I can now say that animists (human or otherwise) move within more-or-less intimate communities assuming that each encounter makes a difference to how the world of relations keeps emerging and, therefore, they seek to interact respectfully (carefully and constructively) and gratefully.

Having said some things about Modernity and animisms, there are two questions to pose: 'What could the collocation "sacred nature" mean for determined Moderns?' and 'What could the collocation "sacred nature" mean for determined animists?' Consideration of these matters could indicate further directions for debates about 'sacred nature' in antiquity.

Remembering that Modernity is no more monolithic than other interacting ways of moving through the world in which many worlds are possible, let us consider where or how a determined Modern might make 'sacred nature'. First, there is the problem of what 'sacred' could mean if religion is really private to individuals and life really secular. Perhaps 'sacred' takes on the role of a synonym of 'special' rather than 'separated', 'access restricted' or 'of heightened value'. But perhaps it is enough that access to some places requires special behaviours – for instance, picnics are only rarely deemed appropriate at the foot of national memorials. Then, if 'Nature' really is entirely composed of 'passive and inert' matter on which form is imposed 'by an agent with a particular end or goal in mind' (Ingold 2013, 213), then bits of it can only be made sacred for solely human ends. (Who else but humans has ends or goals in mind except in fiction?)

Assuming a metaphorical and still powerful use of 'sacred' and a de-animated use of 'Nature', we can observe that Moderns sacralize made-places, human constructions or artefacts, such as war memorials, national monuments, flags, parks and statuary evocative of heritage and productive of citizenship (see, for instance, Chidester and Linenthal 1995). The passive materiality of such places is given the job of symbolising or representing the cherished beliefs and ambitions of particular groups of people. New jobs can be assigned when heritages are re-assessed, as when the statues of slave-traders or despots have been moved to museums and required to tell more critical or more complex stories about previously celebrated pasts and people. Sacralized objects can also be recycled back to their constituent (passive and inert) matter, as when statues and memorials are re-used as (mere) building materials. 'Natural' places identifiable as Modernity's 'sacred nature' can do the same kind of jobs and suffer the same kind of fates. National parks and putative wilderness zones can be sacralized by the removal or control of human inhabitants and the erasure of at least some signs of human activities such as settlements or horticulture. De-sacralisation can involve being handed over to extractive industries for logging, mining or meat production.

If it takes mind to impose form on matter, understanding this *Modern* 'sacred nature' requires consideration of what makes a being human. Modernity has made 'Man' by intensifying interiority and privileging 'rationality'. Martin Luther's 'justification by faith alone', René Descartes 'I think therefore I am', the Westphalian privatisation of religion (Cavanaugh 2009), and Jungian 'individuation' exemplify trajectories and processes which variously create, encapsulate and solidify the Modern person as an individual with – or rather *as* – a definitive interiority. The magical ingredients which need to be added to bodied, sensual materiality to achieve Modernity's belief in an interiority ontology might, as noted above, be labelled soul, spirit, mind, intentionality, agency and so on. The Modern 'believe in belief' (Latour 2015) supports debates and worries about 'relativism' as a way of dealing with the existence of cultural and religious diversity. Indeed, the determined Westphalian/Modern reforming of religion as 'belief' and religionists as 'believers' does not stand alone but illustrates a way of thinking about humans and how they relate to 'others' (Asad 1993; Pietz 1993; Lopez 1998; Latour 2015; Orsi 2015). That is, 'belief' has become definitive not only of religion, or even of all religious and non-religious ideologies or 'world*views*', but also provides a key to recognising the importance of individuality and interiority in this world.

So, how do these interiorized humans generate and engage with 'sacred nature' in practice? One contemporary trend, accentuated during the Covid pandemic, has been to encourage engagement with or immersion in Nature for improving mental health. A slightly longer trend has involved the development of pilgrimage – whether along traditional or new routes – as activities explicitly open to multiple individually tailored justifications and expectations. Mindfulness practices are sometimes presented as most beneficial if conducted outdoors, as when they cross-over into Forest Bathing. People are encouraged to 'find themselves' and/or their 'creativity' by spending significant time in woods or in 'wild places'. In this context, selves and creativity are inner realities and processes – so that, for example, creativity is distinguishable from productivity. Pragmatic or secularized benefits (*e.g.*, better mental health) can be hardly distinguishable from those achieved in 'spiritual' pursuits. All these activities could perhaps happen anywhere but tend to occur in places valorized by particular communities or cultural subgroups. The nub of the matter is that people often go to 'sacred nature' places for inner-self related benefits. They might hug trees or talk to bees but less commonly expect or invite trees to give gifts or bees to initiate conversations. This is not to belittle inner-self focused activities: they are increasingly necessary for those coping with the pressures of trying to be (more) Modern or simply trying to survive. This being so, 'sacred nature' is not a distraction, escape or challenge – it is neither postmodern nor radical but an enabler of Modern personhood and reality. It is a facet of that one-world world, drawing in other possibilities and harnessing them to the task of making a world with inhabitants ready to be more Modern.

If Modernity makes the term 'sacred nature' difficult because, in its reality, only human interiority is supposed to be vital, a different wall of problems is raised for animists. Succinctly: is there a place or even a community usefully called 'Nature'? And, if there is, is it separate from anywhere else? If all places are equally interactive, co-creative communities, are some places 'more equal' than others? Can there be sacred places in worlds where everywhere and everybody deserves respect? There is no singular Nature and there is certainly nothing inert or impassive about the matter of animist worlds. There is only participation and interaction, or relationships. Adapting the meme 'turtles all the way down' I propose that there are hedgehogs – or wombats or mugwort – all the way around. And within that all embracing participative cosmos, indeed composing it with shimmering improvisations, some relations are closer than others. Some kinships are more immediate and make more insistent demands for mutual and sometimes reciprocal response. Animist worlds are not flat or undifferentiated – they can involve the construal of some places (and people and activities) as more important than others. Thus, if I briefly allow myself to say 'nature' in hushed tones, without capitalisation but with those scare quotes, I might say that animists *can* engage with some places as 'sacred nature'. This would mean, again, that as some relations are distinguishable from others, so some places require different (inter-)actions, different etiquette, different care, than others.

Sometimes it is good to go elsewhere to gain insights both into what we know we do not yet know and about what we think we already know. Māori and other Oceanic enacted knowledge have generously gifted the wider world(s) with words helpful in understanding the world in which many worlds are possible. When Captain Cook and his crews returned from his Oceanic/Pacific journeys, they brought back the word 'taboo' (*tapu* or *kapu* in trans-Oceanic dialects). Like other cargo (a word I use with some irony given its misuse in relation to Melanesian economies), it has been adopted in Europe and beyond. Elsewhere I have proposed that 'taboo' might help us rethink religion(s) more dynamically, fluidly, materially, bodily and relationally (Harvey 2013, also see Tremlett 2020). In particular, it could release words like 'sacred' and 'holy' from the stasis imposed on them by a stronger form of dualism than they once carried. Taboo is insistently dynamic and relational. It does not have an *absolute* opposite – but neither did 'sacred' once. Places, people, acts and things can be made sacred, taboo, holy, or (in Hebrew) *qadosh*. And these processes can be reversed. Indeed, Māori hosts who have generously guested me have had to remove *tapu* from me and themselves in order for us to meet, eat, share and otherwise interact. First encounters necessarily bring tabooed differences into proximity. Negotiation and the following of well tested protocols lift *tapu* so that life and living can unfurl and increase.

A short passage from Captain Cook's writing shows that he had also learnt this:

> When dinner was served, not one of [his hosts] would even sit down, or eat a morsel of any thing, as they were all *taboo*, they said; which word, though it has a comprehensive meaning, generally signifies that a thing is prohibited (Cook [1777] 1967, 3.1.129)

As a shared meal had been prepared and was then enjoyed, it is clear not only that prohibitions were lifted but that hosts and guests already knew that taboo was not a permanent, fixed state. Food and eating together are only prohibited until they are not prohibited. Locals and strangers are only *tapu* to each other until they become hosts and guests – always guided by local protocols. Similarly, places are only taboo until the right protocols allow entry. Equally, all these relational interactions require those involved to learn, adopt and abide by the appropriate local etiquette. Sacrality is like this. It is not fixed in opposition to profanity but dynamically interacts with it. Places, people, acts and things can be sacralized or profaned in more-or-less fluid, lumpy or sticky processes (see Mol 2002).

This all allows me to say confidently that places can be made sacred or profane. However, I remain far-more-than-hesitant to call any of these places 'Nature'. This is not only because, so far, the places I have noted have been ones in which human-to-human interactions dominate: places where some humans dwell and others visit, and places where hosts and guests eat together. More significantly, there is no separate, inert realm of 'Nature' further from those meeting and eating places. There are only more persons, kin or potential kin – but of that 'other-than-human' kind. For instance, among Indigenous people as diverse as Māori and Quechua, mountains are relatives. Some are ancestors. Others are rulers (or 'owners of the will'; de la Cadena 2015). They might be immobile (or usually seem so at the speed of human lives) but they are not unmotivated or inactive. They are not waiting to attract beliefs. They have no need to symbolize or represent something significant to human (or eagle or eel) social life. They are already socialising, participating, interacting – at least with some kin and companions.

Nonetheless, a danger in this presentation of animisms is that in emphasising pervasive relationality it might forget Kiiwiich's response to Hallowell: 'no, but *some* are'. Some relations are closer and more pleasant than others (remembering that enmity is a relationship too). Although nowhere is less 'natural' than elsewhere (even if some are less biodiverse than others), some places are treated, engaged with, or raise different expectations than others. Again, while all stones, beavers, hummingbirds, pine trees *could* share gifts, wisdom, time, company, only *some* do so deliberately, significantly or wilfully with some others, sometimes. There are places (living communities) *who* (not 'which') are more regularly visited, or engaged with more certain expectations of conversation, learning and other initiations. Animists might move through the living world knowing that any existence might communicate, might desire company or solitude, might want or resent contact. Learning to be more animistic involves learning how to behave in company, getting to the point where the fact of being and becoming among other animate beings is fully embraced and even casually assumed. But *sometimes* more powerful, more impactful, more immediate things happen. An eagle flies a perfect circle above a drum group at the high point of Mi'kmaq ceremony (Harvey 2017, 100–1). Clouds clear from the night sky at the high point of a British ceremony honouring the 'great bear of the north' (Harvey 2020a; 2020b). Silence while tapping sugar maples leads to closer conversations with other-than-human kin (Gross 2014). Then and there animists could, perhaps, acknowledge that they are standing on sacred ground as part of their story-telling and part of the enhancement of their 'skilful connection-work [of] participative cooperation' (Bird-David 2020). These places, then, could be 'sacred nature' within the pervasive 'more-than-human sociality' or 'biosociality' (Ingold and Palsson 2013; Tsing 2013) of animist worlds.

Actually there is a bit of backtracking to be done before turning to ancient worlds. The world in which many worlds are possible is messier than my presentation may have suggested. It needs saying that Modernity is also relational, changeable, fluid, dynamic and is not separated from animist and other worlds. Bruno Latour's assertion that 'we have never been modern' (1993) has not stopped him writing about what 'Moderns' do and think – and I have followed him. But one of the ways in which Moderns have never been modern is in continuing to enjoy relationships with(in) larger than human kin groups. We converse with some animals, swear at computers, name cars, celebrate encounters with places that grab our attention, refresh our minds, rest our bodies. Recreation might not precisely mean re-creation – but in places that refuse to be 'Nature' Moderns too can find themselves re-made, re-connected, re-invigorated and at least invited to re-kindle kinship through skilled kin-making and maintaining (Bird David 2020). Put differently, Modernity is a construct, a fantasy. It is not a lived reality, or not one that is ever fully realized, bordered, purified. It is an effort, a project. Animisms can be resistance movements against the human separatism of Modernity – but it is enabled in its task by the fact that Moderns are not and cannot be fully Modern – they/we are already on a journey to animism or other possible worlds, none of which is ever actually separate. For example, people move within *and* between Modernity and animisms with more or less ease or discomfort. They can seek mental health and spiritual wellbeing/holism while communing with plants or giving thanks to food persons. Despite etymologies that require cutting apart of sacred and profane places, people and acts, 'sacred nature' is always available. Perhaps what this all means is that we have always been animists but have tried to become Moderns – making efforts to de-animate and objectify the world(s) while depriving ourselves and others of relatedness (see Hornborg 2006). But the resistance is growing – in a post-Cartesian academia and in other worlds.

Although most of my research has been focused either on contemporary animisms or on the legacies of early-modern reforming (privatisation and de-materialisation) of religion, these contexts provide lenses for re-viewing ancient worlds. I think we can be confident that no one in any ancient world was a Modern. However, whether they were animists or not, an understanding of the relationality that is key to current animist worlds and world-making invites reflection on what such people said, wrote, built, ate, ritualized, imagined, venerated and done in many other ways. The 'relational turn' of new animism cannot but enhance research and teaching about antiquity which engages with gendered, material, anti-colonial, sensual, and other vital foci. For example, many scholars (collaborating in the resistance against Modernity) have not only recognized but contested the reclassification of 'the entire field of ancient and contemporary religious phenomena' as a *problem* of materiality or physicality (Pietz 1993, 138). This resistance must involve rejecting the idea that there is an

> absolute split between the mechanistic-material realm of physical nature (the blind determinism of whose events excluded any principle of teleological causality, that is, Providence) and the end-orientated human realm of purposes and desires (whose free intentionality distinguished its events as moral action, properly determined by rational ideals rather than by the material contingency of merely natural being). (Pietz 1993, 139)

Recovering (new) materialists rediscover relationality. In doing so they re-skill in 'an art of noticing [which] is not learning to see things differently, but learning to see different things' (Savransky 2021, 42). It is not that Modernists and animists see mountains, stones, eagles, hedgehogs or 'nature' differently. Rather, one community sees 'Nature' where the others see communities of kin. These are different. An inert mountain is not the same as an ancestor mountain. A merely instinctual, blindly determined eagle is not the same as an eagle who expresses delight when humans join in rituals honouring life. Naming these different things – and their differences – confers 'on what is named the power to make us feel and think in the mode that name calls for' (Stengers 2015, 43). The shapes thrown at us by the world might be the same, but the beings are different. In 'Nature' mountains (scenery) and humans (observers) are separable. In the animate world mountains-and-humans become together. This is a difference that not only makes a difference but makes more worlds possible.

Such possibilities raise interesting questions about the worlds of ancient peoples. Recent scholarship about four ancient cultural contexts encourages further experiments with the application of 'new animism' and related approaches. Those contexts are Palaeolithic rock art, Mesopotamian cosmology, Hebrew Bible environmental ethics and Roman religion. Brief examples indicate some of the directions already taken. Robert Wallis has proposed that Palaeolithic art in the Lascaux cave (in the Dordogne, France) 'was active in the pragmatic negotiation of hunter-shaman practice' (Wallis 2021, 332; also see Wallis 2009; Wallis and Carocci 2021). He fuses research about the animist ontologies and mimetic practices of hunter-gatherers, and about the work of the shamans they often employ, to enrich understanding and advance debate. Laura Feldt (2016) and Anna Perdibon (2019; 2020) have demonstrated the value of reading diverse ancient Mesopotamian texts through the lens of animism. Mountains, rivers, birds and other beings – including deities – interact (supportively or adversarially) with both humans and other-than-humans in a relational cosmos. Similarly, Mari Joerstad (2019) shows how an animist reading of Hebrew Bible texts escapes the imposition of a Modern ontology that turns references to other-than-human interactions into mere metaphors. Taken seriously, texts throughout the bible insist on respectful inter-relationships between humans and the larger-than-human world and the larger cosmos. Emma-Jayne Graham's (2021) 'reassembling' of religion in ancient Rome leads me to think ancient Roman religion could also be called animistic. She concludes that

> temporary and situationally specific relationships between humans and more-than-human things were crucial for the performance and experience of Roman religion as lived, and for the subsequent production of both distal and proximal forms of religious knowledge. (Graham 2021, 201)

Her detailed presentation of multiple examples of such relationships encourages further resistance (as scholars and other kinds of kin) against Modernity's project of de-animating 'Nature' and of depriving we humans of relatedness so that we can become more fully individuated or 'Cartesians' (Hornborg 2006, 28). Other possibilities open to us, again as (inter- or un-)disciplined scholars and as participants in a larger-than-human world.

There is an added importance to seeking to understand ancient 'sacred nature' or ancient relations with(in) the larger-than-human world. That is, that such seeking takes (makes) place in a dangerous time. Nature 'has left behind its traditional role and now has the power to question us all' and Gaia, now 'offended', demands that we experiment 'with the possibilities of manners of living and cooperating that have been destroyed in the name of progress' (Stengers 2015, 12, 158). Whether Gaia will reward our experiments is far from the point (Stengers is clear that this will not happen). Nonetheless, experiments derived from better understanding of ancient and contemporary worlds in a world in which many worlds are possible must be worth the effort if we are to make not only more but also more liveable shared worlds.

References

Abram, D. (1996) *The Spell of the Sensuous: perception and language in a more-than-human world.* New York, Pantheon Books.

Asad, T. (1993) *Genealogies of Religion: discipline and reasons of power in Christianity and Islam.* Baltimore MD, Johns Hopkins University Press.

Bhambra, G.K. (2007) *Rethinking Modernity: postcolonialism and the sociological imagination.* Basingstoke, Palgrave Macmillan.

Bird-David, N. (2018) Persons or relatives? Animistic scales of practice and imagination. In M. Astor-Aguilera and G. Harvey (eds) *Rethinking Personhood: Animism and Materiality*, 25–34. New York, Routledge.

Bird-David, N. (2020). A peer-to-peer connected cosmos: beyond egalitarian/hierarchical hunter-gatherer societies. *L'Homme* 236 (3), 77–106.

Cavanaugh, W.T. (2009) *The Myth of Religious Violence: Secular Ideology and the Roots of Modern Conflict.* Oxford, Oxford University Press.

Chidester, D. and Linenthal, E.T. (1995) *American Sacred Space.* Bloomington IN, Indiana University Press.

Cook, J. [1777] (1967) *A Journal of a Voyage Round the World in HMS Endeavour 1768–1771.* New York, Da Capo Press.

de la Cadena, M. (2015) *Earth Beings: ecologies of practice across Andean worlds.* Durham NC, Duke University Press.

de la Cadena, M. and Blaser, M. (2018) *A World of Many Worlds.* Durham NC, Duke University Press.

Descola, P. (2014) All too human (still) a comment on Eduardo Kohn's How forests think. *HAU: Journal of Ethnographic Theory* 4 (2), 267–273.

Escobar, A. (2020) *Pluriversal Politics: the read and the possible.* Durham NC, Duke University Press.

Feldt, L. (2016) Religion, nature, and ambiguous space in ancient Mesopotamia: The mountain wilderness in Old Babylonian religious narratives. *Numen* 63, 347–382.

Gibson, K., Bird Rose, D. and Fincher, R. (2015) *Manifesto for Living in the Anthropocene.* New York, Punctum Books.

Graham, E.-J. (2021) *Reassembling Religion in Roman Italy.* London, Routledge.

Gross, L.W. (2014) *Anishinaabe Ways of Knowing and Being.* New York, Routledge.

Hallowell, A.I. (1960) Ojibwa ontology, behavior, and world view. In S. Diamond (ed.) *Culture in History*, 19–52. New York, Columbia University Press.

Haraway, D. (1988) Situated knowledges: the science question in feminism and the privilege of partial perspective. *Feminist Studies* 14 (3), 575–599.

Haraway, D. (2015) Anthropocene, capitalocene, plantationocene, chthulucene: making kin. *Environmental Humanities* 6, 159–165.

Harvey, G. (2013) *Food, Sex and Strangers: understanding religion as everyday life*. London, Routledge.

Harvey, G. (2017) *Animism: Respecting the Living World*. London, Hurst (2nd revised edn).

Harvey, G. (2020a) Trans-indigenous festivals, democracy and emplacement. In S. Pike, J. Salomonsen and P.-F. Tremlett (eds) *Ritual and Democracy: protests, publics and performances*, 139–159. Sheffield, Equinox.

Harvey, G. (2020b) Bear feasts in a land without (wild) bears: experiments in creating animist rituals. In G. Harvey (ed.) *Indigenizing in European Religious Movements*, 31–49. Sheffield, Equinox.

Hogan, L. (2013) We call it *tradition* in G. Harvey (ed.) *The Handbook of Contemporary Animism*, 17–26. New York, Routledge.

Hornborg, A. (2006) Animism, fetishism, and objectivism as strategies for knowing (or not knowing) the world. *Ethnos* 71 (1), 21–32.

Ingold, T. (2006) Rethinking the animate, re-animating thought. *Ethnos* 71 (1), 9–20.

Ingold, T (2013) Being alive to a world without objects. In G. Harvey (ed.) *The Handbook of Contemporary Animism*, 2123–2125 New York, Routledge.

Ingold, T. and Palsson, G. eds (2013) *Biosocial Becomings: integrating social and biological anthropology*. Cambridge, Cambridge University Press.

Joerstad, M. (2019) *The Hebrew Bible and Environmental Ethics*. Cambridge, Cambridge University Press.

Kimmerer, R.W. (2013) *Braiding Sweetgrass: indigenous wisdom, scientific knowledge, and the teachings of plants*. Minneapolis MN, Milkweed.

Kimmerer, R.W. (2015) Nature needs a new pronoun: to stop the age of extinction, let's start by ditching 'it'. *Yes Magazine*, https://www.yesmagazine.org/issue/together-earth/2015/03/30/alternative-grammar-a-new-language-of-kinship (accessed 27 March 2022).

King, T. (2003) *The Truth about Stories: a native narrative*. Minneapolis MN, University of Minnesota Press.

Latour, B. (1993) *We Have Never Been Modern*. New York, Harvester Wheatsheaf.

Latour, B. (2015) Fetish-factish. In S. Brent Plante (ed.) *Key Terms in Material Religion*, 87–94. London, Bloomsbury.

Law, J. (1994) *Organizing Modernity*. Oxford, Blackwell.

Law, J. (2004) *After Method: mess in social science research*. London, Routledge.

Law, J. (2015) What's wrong with a one-world world? *Distinktion: Journal of Social Theory* 16 (1), 126–139.

Law, J. (2019) Material semiotics. URL: http://heterogeneities.net/publications/Law2019MaterialSemiotics.pdf (Accessed 25 Mar 2022).

Lopez, D. (1998) Belief. In M.C. Taylor (ed.) *Critical Terms for Religious Studies*, 21–35. Chicago IL, University of Chicago Press.

Marcos, Subcomandante [Vicente, R.S.G.] (1996) *EZLN Fourth Declaration of the Lacandon Jungle*, III. https://schoolsforchiapas.org/wp-content/uploads/2014/03/Fourth-Declaration-of-the-Lacandona-Jungle-.pdf (accessed 25 Mar 2022).

Matthews, M. and Roulette, R. (2018) Are all stone alive?: anthropological and Anishinaabe approaches to personhood. In M. Astor-Aguilera and G. Harvey (eds) *Rethinking Personhood: animism and materiality*, 173–192. New York, Routledge.

Merleau-Ponty, M. (1962) *Phenomenology of Perception*. London, Routledge & Kegan Paul.

Mol, A. (2002) *The Body Multiple: ontology in medical practice*. Durham NC: Duke University Press.

Naveh, D. and Bird-David, N. (2013) Animism, conservation and immediacy. In G. Harvey (ed.) *The Handbook of Contemporary Animism*, 27–37. New York, Routledge.

Orsi, R. (2015) Belief. In S. Brent Plante (ed.) *Key Terms in Material Religion*, 17–23. London, Bloomsbury.

Perdibon, A. (2019) *Mountains and Trees, Rivers and Springs. animistic beliefs and practices in ancient Mesopotamian religion*. Wiesbaden, Harrassowitz.

Perdibon, A. (2020) Nature as conceived by the Mesopotamians and the current anthropological debate over animism and personhood. The case of Ebiḫ: mountain, person and god. *Distant Worlds Journal* 4, 124–136.

Piercy, M. (1979) *Woman on the Edge of Time*. London, Women's Press.

Pietz, W. (1993) Fetishism and materialism: the limits of theory in Marx. In E. Apter and W. Pietz (eds) *Fetishism as Cultural Discourse*, 119–151. Ithaca NY, Cornell University Press.

Povinelli, E.A. (2016) *Geontologies: a requiem to late Liberalism*. Durham NC, Duke University Press.

Savransky, M. (2021) *Around the Day in Eighty Worlds: politics of the pluriverse*. Durham NC, Duke University Press.

Stengers, I. (2015) *In Catastrophic Times: resisting the coming barbarism*. Lüneberg, Meson Press.

Tsing, A.L. (2013) More than human sociality. *Anthropology and Nature* 14, 27–42.

Tremlett, P. (2020) *Towards a New Theory of Religion and Social Change: sovereignties and disruptions*. London, Bloomsbury.

Wallis, R.J. (2009) Re-enchanting rock art landscapes: animic ontologies, nonhuman agency and rhizomic personhood. *Time and Mind: The Journal of Archaeology, Consciousness and Culture* 2 (1), 47–70.

Wallis, R. J. (2021) Hunters and shamans, sex and death: relational ontologies and the materiality of the Lascaux 'shaft-scene'. In O.M. Abadía and M. Porr (eds) *Ontologies of Rock Art: images, relational approaches and indigenous knowledge*, 319–333. Abingdon: Routledge.

Wallis, R.J. and Carocci, M. (2021) iIntroduction to the Special Issue Art, Shamanism and Animism. *Religions* 12, 853.

Chapter 2

Watercraft as assemblage in the Western Arctic

Erica Hill

Watercraft, like amulets and harpoons, were critical components of the maritime North American Arctic toolkit. Two forms of skin-covered watercraft were in use across the Western Arctic: the umiaq, a large open boat, and the smaller, decked kayak. Comprised of driftwood and animal skins and constructed through the complementary labour of men and women, watercraft mediated the realms of land, ice and water, operating as liminal agents between human and animal worlds. This chapter explores watercraft of the Western Arctic coast as hybrid assemblages of raw materials that were themselves implicated in relational networks. Inspired by McNiven's (2018) view of Torres Strait canoes as 'object-beings,' I consider the evidence of the Late Thule and early contact period in Alaska and the islands of the Bering Sea (ca. CE 1400–1850). Routine watercraft construction and maintenance, from this perspective, become complex social processes that transform, renew and connect humans, animals and materials (driftwood, seal skins) with their own agential properties.

Nineteenth-century Indigenous peoples living along the coasts of the Bering and Chukchi seas possessed sophisticated maritime toolkits that enabled them to hunt and survive on land, sea and ice. Skin-covered watercraft were essential components of those toolkits, used for travel, transport and hunting. Two forms were common in the North Pacific: the *umiaq*, a large open boat, and the smaller, decked *qayaq* (or kayak). This chapter explores the skin boat as one node in a complex relational network that linked humans and marine mammals, their primary prey. Below, I suggest that construction of the *umiaq* and its associated technologies materialized social relations between men and women, and among humans, plants and animals. In use, the *umiaq* operated as a liminal agent between human and animal worlds, a role of immense symbolic power. After a brief discussion of the gendered social values embedded in *umiaq* construction and ownership, I suggest that the *umiaq* might be productively thought of as an 'object-being' (*sensu* McNiven 2018) operative in the relational network connecting humans and whales. I further suggest that the *umiaq*, like other complex forms of material culture, was a hybrid assemblage of affordances, implicated in familial, social, economic, and technological networks connecting humans with a host of other agents.

The *umiaq* as assemblage

The coasts of the Bering and Chukchi seas (Fig. 2.1) are the traditional homelands of the Inupiat of northern and western Alaska, and two groups of Yupik-speaking peoples – the Yupiit of Southwest Alaska and the Yupiget of St Lawrence Island and the Chukchi Peninsula. Here I use the term 'Yupiit' to refer to all speakers of Yupik languages, distinguishing them from the Inupiat, who are linguistically more closely related to Inuit of Canada and Kalaallit of Greenland. As inhabitants of islands and coasts, Inupiat and Yupiit developed sophisticated understandings of prey animals, primarily marine mammals and birds. Several lines of ethnohistoric and archaeological

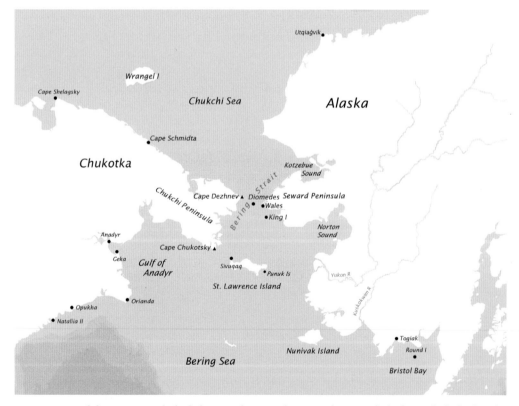

Fig. 2.1: *Map of the Bering and Chukchi seas showing the coastal areas of Alaska and Chukotka, the traditional homelands of the Inupiat and Yupiit in the 19th century.*

evidence indicate that some marine mammals were perceived as persons who lived in societies parallel to those of humans. These animals, including seals, walrus, whales and beluga, played key roles in complex relational networks that linked men and women, human families, other-than-human persons, and humans to animals (Hill 2011; 2012).

Hunting on sea or ice was one form of interaction between humans and marine mammals. As I have suggested elsewhere (Hill 2013), hunting in many hunter-gatherer societies was considerably more complicated than a single encounter in which an animal was killed. Rather, hunting may be considered a series of activities that involved husbands and wives working cooperatively, and their relations with prey. At least on the human side, there was recognition of animal agency and intention, and the sense that animals were aware of human thought, speech and behaviour. In recognition of this awareness, humans in the Bering Sea region took care with what they said about animals and how they prepared clothing and hunting equipment. Both men and women observed rules of behaviour, or etiquette, for dealing with animals before, during and after the hunt.

Whaling was perhaps the most socially, technologically and ritually complex form of hunting by Bering Sea coastal inhabitants. Whaling was made possible by a technological suite that included harpoons, floats, blades, and watercraft. At historic contact in the 18th and 19th centuries, Inupiat and Yupiit employed two types of watercraft, both constructed of driftwood frames covered by marine mammal skins. The *qayaq* (kayak) was primarily used by single hunters, while the *umiaq* was a larger, open boat used for hunting, travel and transport (Murdoch 1892, 328–338; Nelson 1899, 216–222; Anichtchenko 2020). Hunting by *umiaq* was a communal affair, and targeted large marine mammals, primarily bowhead whales (*Balaena mysticetus*), grey whales (*Eschrichtius robustus*) and walrus (*Odobenus rosmarus*). The term *umiaq* (plural *umiat*) is Inupiaq; on St Lawrence Island, these boats are known as *angyapik* (pl. *angyapiget*) (Braund 1988).

Direct archaeological evidence for Arctic watercraft prior to the Thule period (ca. CE 1200–1400) is literally fragmentary with the *qayaq* significantly pre-dating the *umiaq*. Pieces from the earliest securely dated *umiaq* frames, known from northern Alaska, date to about CE 1000. They originated at the Birnirk type site (Anichtchenko 2016, 224) and the Birnirk component of the Rising Whale site at Cape Espenberg (Alix *et al.* 2018). A third site, Deering, yielded an *umiaq* headboard from the Thule component. Identified as spruce wood (*Picea* sp.), the piece originated at the base of the tree trunk and was likely chosen for its curved shape (Alix 2009, D60).

Sophisticated watercraft and maritime hunting technologies were likely key to the rapid migration of the Thule people – the predecessors of modern Inuit – across the North American Arctic from the Bering Sea to Greenland, where they were well established by CE 1400 (Friesen 2016; LeMoine and Darwent 2016). As a result, *umiat* were employed prior to contact from the coasts of Chukotka in the west (Ainana *et al.* 2003) to Greenland in the east (Petersen 1986), with local and regional differences in form, construction and use. Given the limited archaeological evidence, our understanding of watercraft use along the Bering and Chukchi sea coasts is dependent primarily upon later ethnohistoric and ethnographic sources (Jensen 2012) which provide analogues for pre-contact boat technologies. Representations of boats in the form of rock art and miniature ivory and birch-bark models, collected or recovered archaeologically, also inform our reconstructions of pre-contact watercraft (for instance, Anichtchenko and Crowell 2010; Anichtchenko 2016, 46–50; Alix *et al.* 2018).

At historic contact and into the first half of the 20th century, *umiat* and *angyapiget* were constructed of wooden frames made of driftwood and then covered with skins of either bearded seal (*Erignathus barbatus*) or walrus (*Odobenus rosmarus*). Lashings, lines, paddles, bailers, harpoon rests, floats and toggles made of hide, sinew, baleen and ivory outfitted the *umiaq*, while the boat captain, steersman and crew provided additional gear, including harpoons and ceremonial objects (Crowell 2009a). Both wood and sea mammal skins were critical resources in Northwest Alaska and St Lawrence Island, much of which is treeless tundra. Wood was exclusively driftwood, primarily spruce (*Picea*) in Alaska, originating in the large river systems of the Yukon, Kuskokwim and Kobuk/Noatak (Alix 2016). Driftwood was a seasonal resource, only available starting in the spring, when rivers thawed and logs arrived downriver. In a tundra environment, the right piece of wood for boat construction might be curated for several generations, signalling access to resources and the expertise of a craftsman, who recognized the value and utility of a specific piece of wood among hundreds. The type of wood, its grain, shape, weight and origin in trunk, stump or root were all considerations in selecting materials for *umiaq* construction (Alix *et al.* 2018).

Sea mammal skins, sewn together to cover the driftwood frame, were similarly prized, demonstrating both hunting success and the ability to acquire a surplus. Not all seal or walrus skins were appropriate for watercraft use. When walrus was used, the skins of adult females were preferred, as they were less scarred and warty than those of males and therefore more flexible with greater tensile strength. Four or five hides were generally required to cover an average-size *umiaq* of about 8 m length. Every two or three years, the boat cover needed to be replaced as it lost resiliency and became damaged through use (Bogojavlensky 1969; Braund 1988).

Procuring either bearded seal or walrus was itself a potentially dangerous, time-consuming and labour-intensive activity. Reaching the ice floes where walrus cows and calves congregate could involve dragging watercraft over several kilometres of rough ice. Hunting success was never assured and, even if an animal was wounded, it could escape or sink before it could be retrieved. Should a crew be successful in acquiring a female walrus, they must still return to shore with their catch. Once the hides of either walrus or bearded seal were procured, men and women co-operated in their processing – a series of time- and energy-intensive steps that involved splitting the hides, removing hair, blubber and flesh and stretching them.

In the 19th century, men were responsible for the collection of driftwood and the construction of the *umiaq* frame. The number and variety of wooden pieces required for an *umiaq* could take several seasons to accumulate – the frame required a keel, gunwales, thwarts, ribs, headboard and seats (Braund 1988). Carving each piece, followed by assembly using scarfed joins and baleen lashing, was often accomplished by older men or a boat-building expert (Anichtchenko 2016, 103). Once the frame was constructed, the prepared skins were laid over the keel (Fig. 2.2). Expert seamstresses then sewed together the prepared skins using watertight seams (Fig. 2.3) before the new cover was stretched over the *umiaq* gunwales and attached.

The initial construction of the *umiaq* and its routine recovering every two or three years required the mobilisation and organisation of the labour of both men and women, generally linked by marriage or kinship, either fictive or biological. The process required several seasons to collect the driftwood and materials from two or three species of marine mammals, including the skins of bearded seal or walrus, ivory fittings from walrus tusk and baleen from bowhead or gray whales. Skins used to cover an *umiaq* were a surplus, beyond the number of seals needed to provide boots and clothing. As suggested at the beginning of this chapter, the *umiaq* was the product of multiple transformational processes that connected men, women, plants and animals. These processes were relational, based upon the co-operative labour

Fig. 2.2: *Men laying skins over an* umiaq *frame, possibly at King Island, Alaska, 1930–1938. Courtesy Alaska State Library, Historical Collections, Kenneth Chisholm Photograph Collection (ASL P105-028).*

Fig. 2.3: Women in northern Alaska sewing bearded sealskins together to cover an umiaq. *Four skins are visible in this photo. The* umiaq *is balanced on two sleds. A sod house appears in the background. Courtesy Alaska State Library, Historical Collections, Rev. Samuel Spriggs Collection, Point Barrow (now Utqiaġvik), Alaska, 1899–1908 (ASL P320-60).*

of husbands and wives, extended families and kin groups. Procurement of the skins was also a relational process, as it required the hunter to be successful – not just in the act of finding and taking an animal, but also in maintaining good relations with prey animals in general. Hunting success was thus determined both by the respectful behaviour of the hunter and by agency and generosity of the seal, whale or walrus. From this perspective, the *umiaq* may be considered a multispecies assemblage of materials and labour.

Fair (2005) has suggested that *umiat* might productively be considered architecture, rather than watercraft *per se*. She emphasized the role of the *umiaq* in social relations, pointing to its complex involvement in the daily lives of the community. When at rest, the *umiaq* might function to define spatial and ethnic boundaries within a village and between residents and others. *Umiat* also materialized the wealth and status the owner (Sheehan 1985; 1995) and the family's ability to mobilize the labour of men to construct the frame, women to prepare and sew the cover and a 6–10 man crew to hunt whale and walrus. This type of communal hunting therefore required the acquisition and possession of wood for an *umiaq* frame, sea mammal skins, lines, toggles, paddles and a host of ritual objects, along with the social capital to mobilize the labour of male and female artisans, and the charisma and management expertise to organize and direct a crew (Ellanna 1988). The term *umialiq* continues in use today to refer to both the boat captain and owner – roles of significant social, economic and ceremonial status. While most 19th-century Yup'ik and Inupiaq men might own a *qayaq*, possessing the social status to construct and outfit an *umiaq* and its crew was less common (Anichtchenko 2016, 124).

Still, ownership of a well-made *umiaq* and the presence of a crew did not ensure hunting success. Also required were good relations between humans and prey animals, particularly whales. Maintenance of good relations between humans and the prey that made the entire whaling enterprise possible, proclaiming an *umialiq's* prowess as a hunter, manager, leader, ritualist and communicator. Women, as both skin sewers and part of the relationship network between humans and prey, were central to the entire process. The *umialiq's* wife, in particular, had a role as critical on land as the *umialiq's* at sea. Her behaviour and leadership before, during and after a hunt determined its success. Her obligations extended to the whale as well as to human community members. She had a plethora of obligations to fulfil and taboo activities to avoid (on Yup'ik practices, see Lantis 1938; Fienup-Riordan 1994; Morrow 2002). During the whaling season, both her thoughts and actions could affect hunting success (Spencer 1959; Bodenhorn 1990). She traditionally provided the whale with its drink of water in acknowledgment of its gift, and she ensured the generous distribution of meat at the celebratory feast and in daily practice. As in the eastern Arctic (Laugrand and Oosten 2015), a stingy wife drove away sea mammals, who sought instead a woman who honoured the spirit of their gift.

An *umiaq* therefore represented not just the status and power of an *umialiq*, but also that of his wife. It materialized an ideal of co-operative gendered labour and encapsulated some of the foundational values of Inupiaq and Yupik society. In material terms, the *umiaq* was constituted from the two realms inhabited by Inupiat, Yupiit and their predecessors: driftwood as a terrestrial and riverine resource, and seal or walrus skins from the sea, plus objects of baleen, ivory and stone. *Umiaq* construction required driftwood with specific properties and the expertise to carve the wood into the keel, headboard, ribs, gunwales, stringers, crosspieces and seats that comprised the frame. The skin covering, sewn by seamstresses to be watertight, strong and flexible, represented multiple seals or walrus, and the time and skill to hunt them, as well as the time to scrape and split the skins, tie and stretch them on wooden frames and, ultimately, assemble them as a cover. Labour to build and cover the *umiaq* was mobilized by an *umialiq* and his wife, who each had specific responsibilities vis-à-vis the crew and the prey animals the crew would hunt (Rainey 1947; Spencer 1959).

As the complex product of labour, skill and expertise, plant and animal lives, and a network of relations linking men and women, kin and non-kin, humans and animals, the *umiaq* may be considered an assemblage – not just an assemblage of materials but also of sense and affect, processes and relations, households and communities, both human and animal (Hamilakis and Jones 2017; Jervis 2019). *Assemblage* is an analytical concept articulated by Gilles Deleuze (Deleuze and Parnet [1977] 1987, 69) as a 'multiplicity' comprised of heterogeneous elements which establish 'liaisons, relations between them, across ages, sexes and reigns – different natures. Thus, the assemblage's only unity is that of co-functioning: it is a symbiosis, a 'sympathy'. It is never filiations which are important, but alliances, alloys'. Müller (2015, 28) clarifies this, writing that an assemblage is 'a mode of ordering heterogeneous entities so that they work together for a certain time'. He describes assemblages as relational, made up of disparate elements, and productive; that is, they produce 'new behaviours, new expressions, new actors, and new realities' (Müller 2015, 28–29). In their construction, assemblages pull together the social and the material, creating new constellations of human, plant, and animal bodies that function in ways distinct from their component parts.

The *umiaq* can be considered a relational assemblage of multiple plant and animal life cycles and their respective characteristics and affordances: 'temporary and deliberate heterogeneous arrangements of material and immaterial elements' (Hamilakis 2017, 169). While a driftwood gunwale made of spruce contributes a certain hardness, weight and tensile strength, the skin of a female walrus covering the bow brings flexibility and resilience, bouncing off the ice edge and resisting tears and waterlogging. The labour of the woman who stretched and sun-bleached the skin to appeal to bowhead whales and that of the seamstress who lapped the seams with watertight stitching were also assembled in the *umiaq*, as were the expertise of the wood-worker and the ceremonial observances of the *umialiq* and the crew. The processes of creating the *umiaq* as a complex, composite artifact, of assembling it as a hybridized entanglement of relations, defies attempts to separate living from non-living, land and sea, nature and culture. The *umiaq* is simultaneously all these characteristics and relations, which emerge and recede in the processes of construction, use and discard. Whitridge (2004) has taken a similar view of the hunting harpoon head which he interprets as part of a hybrid network involving hunter, tool and prey animal. The harpoon has no essential quality; rather it is characterized by 'its liability to be enrolled in an ever-expanding web of social circularity and meaning, like all material culture' (Whitridge 2004, 457).

The particular assemblage of materials and processes that is the *umiaq* is inherently unstable – it acquires a highly contextualized life-history and agency, discussed in greater detail below. In its construction and use, material components of the *umiaq* become worn or damaged and are repaired or replaced. Bogojavlensky (1969, 244) draws an analogy between the condition of the *umiaq* cover and the crew, which he interpreted as a political faction, writing 'When the skins of a boat rot away, it is a sign that a faction has disintegrated' and the political landscape, featuring the *umialiq*, has shifted. Wear and tear mark the watercraft's history of use, its encounters with sea ice, mishap or carelessness. The human crew gains or loses members, the season changes, and walrus and whales are hunted, taken or lost, butchered and shared.

The *umialiq* acquires status (or does not), and his wife behaves generously (or she does not). All these entities, actions and processes adhere through memory to the *umiaq* and become its assembled life history, unique and localised in time and space. Simultaneously, the *umiaq* acts as an agent itself, an animated 'object-being' mediating relations between human and animal communities.

The *umiaq* as agent and object-being

In his study of Torres Strait watercraft, McNiven (2018) identifies canoes as animate and predatory 'object-beings'. This term appears to be equally applicable to the northern *umiaq*. Like the Thule, Inupiat and Yupiit of Alaska, the Torres Strait Islanders of northeast Australia have long been marine specialists with complex relationships with prey animals, both living and dead. Their canoes were embedded in human social networks as agents, animated and socialized 'to become active and useful members of Torres Strait Islander communities' (McNiven 2018, 186). The canoes were understood as bodies, emerging from trees, engendered and transformed through human labour. McNiven describes a process of anthropo- and zoomorphising the watercraft, attributing anatomical features to bow, hull and stern. The bow or 'head' possessed eyes capable of seeing prey and a mouth with teeth of shell attachments (McNiven 2018, 176–182). A highly salient feature of these canoes was their desire to hunt, accentuated by carving or painting predatory fish on the bow or stern. The names of the canoes also contributed to the expression of predatory agency, referencing poisonous snakes and piscivorous birds (McNiven 2018, 185). McNiven (2018, 170) writes that, as other-than-human beings, and potentially persons, object-beings should not be seen as 'accessories' to humans, but as 'social partners, actors, and participants in human action and broader social arenas'.

McNiven's characterisation of watercraft as 'object-beings' fits the ethnohistoric descriptions of Alaska *umiat*, though *umiat* differ from Torres Strait canoes in some respects. Like canoes, though, *umiat* appear to have been animated and agential, apparently enlivened through the process of construction and the actions of the *umialiq*, his wife and crew. Like *umiat*, canoes and other watercraft throughout Melanesia were implicated in human gender relations. They were also part of a series of processes that transformed a tree trunk into a canoe, awakened it, and established a sympathetic connection between the canoe and its builder (McNiven 2018, 177–178). Below I discuss the evidence that supports the interpretation of the *umiaq* as an animated 'object-being' and identify some of the similarities and differences that emerge from a comparison between *umiat* and Melanesian canoes.

The *umiaq* and the use of amulets

Both kayaks and *umiat* often contained amulets installed in their wooden frames (Anichtchenko 2016). Like personal amulets possessed by humans (and some dogs), a boat amulet might convey certain animal traits to a boat. This parallel use of amulets by both humans and *umiat* suggests that agency, and possibly personhood, was attributed to watercraft. Like amulets used by humans, boat amulets operated by linking two animate, or agential, entities: the watercraft and the animal embodied by the amulet. The notion of the *umiaq* as an agent is conveyed in some traditional narratives; one recorded by Rasmussen (Ostermann and Holtved 1952, 262) in northern Alaska describes the origins of boat amulets. There was a girl who could not find a husband. Her father built an *umiaq* for her and drew a bird on the side and a salmon on the bottom. The bird amulet would allow the *umiaq* to rise above the water when great speed was needed or cruise smoothly along the surface as a salmon. The girl set off and eventually she spied a settlement where she found the son of an *umialiq*. They married and, since then, these types of amulets have been used on all *umiat*.

In this story, the *umiaq* is described as an agent, transforming itself into a bird or a salmon, deciding to swim upriver and resting onshore. The *umiaq*, not the girl, receives the powers conveyed by the animal amulets, suggesting that it possessed its own spirit and capacities which could be enhanced or supplemented with those of animals. In Northwest Alaska, Ray (1885, 39) reported the use of wolf skulls, raven and eagle skins, 'for no boat would be considered equipped without some such talisman'. Murdoch (1892, 437–438) reported the use of stuffed ravens and eagles and added fox tails and eagle feathers to the list of *umiaq* 'charms'. He collected a stuffed godwit (Scolopacidae), a large shorebird with a long and distinctive bill, specifically used for whaling, which was mounted on a stick. His description of the bird as 'soiled and ragged' suggests that it was being discarded, having served for the season. Stuffed birds were also reportedly part of a cache of early 19th-century whaling gear discovered on Sledge Island in 1912 (Kaplan *et al.* 1984).

Yup'ik speakers in Southwest Alaska also used birds as watercraft amulets. On Nunivak Island dried cranes were among the objects placed in a kayak at its first launch (Collins 1927). Curtis (1930, 15–16) indicates that boat amulets could be either painted representations or animal parts. Most of the birds used as amulets are those proficient at diving and fishing, including ducks, cormorants, loons and grebes. Curtis explained that the people of Nunivak painted animals on watercraft in the belief that 'the spirit-power of the animal will become embodied in the kaiak [*i.e.*, *qayaq*] and aid materially in catching game'.

McNiven (2018, 183–184) reports that Torres Strait Islanders also used 'hunting magic charms', which were either carried onboard the canoes or were attached to the interior. Carved images or body parts of two species of marine birds (sea eagles and frigate birds) were often used, both known as 'voracious catchers of fish'. The use of hunting birds as amulets in both Alaska and Torres Strait suggests that the watercraft were intended to harness the birds' abilities and enhance the hunting success of their human crews. This use of amulets blurs distinctions among the agencies of humans, animals and animated objects, creating new hybrid assemblages of traits and behaviours.

The umiaq and rites of passage

In the spring, whaling communities prepared for the hunt by general refurbishment of whaling implements, cleaning of meat caches, dances, chants and songs and new clothing (Rainey 1947; Spencer 1959, 332; Crowell 2009a). Several days or weeks would be devoted to ritual activities and observance of prohibitions involving the *umialiq*, his wife and the *umiaq* crew. At the village of Wales, on the Seward Peninsula, the recovered *umiaq* was smoke purified and the boat captain and harpooner kept vigil with the watercraft overnight (Curtis 1930, 140), possibly to prevent ritual sabotage, a practice reported by Silook for St Lawrence Island (1917a, 109). In addition to refurbished tools, a new *umiaq* cover and new clothes, acts of renewal could include the installation of a new bird amulet in the *umiaq* (Lantis 1947, 40). Spring was also when some communities celebrated boat launching ceremonies.

Boat launching may be likened to a rite of passage, 'waking up' the watercraft (Lowenstein 1993, 139) and initiating its role in the whaling enterprise. At Point Hope, the wife of a whaling captain is described as giving the boat a drink from a special vessel (Rainey 1947, 257). Yupik historian Paul Silook of St Lawrence Island described the boat captain 'feeding' the *umiaq* when the crew feasted (Silook 1917b, 90–91). Elsewhere he writes that a captain might admonish the *umiaq* that it 'should be beautiful [in] the sight of the whale' (Silook 1937, 38). These descriptions are reminiscent of Rasmussen's story of the *umiaq* accompanying the girl looking for a husband in which the craft is treated as an agent capable of actively assisting the girl in her search. McNiven (2018, 186, 187) describes similar rites practised in Melanesia where canoes were awakened either during their initial construction or prior to hunting expeditions. He considers these rites to be acts of socialisation in which the inherent animacy and agency of the watercraft was activated through human engagement.

Recovering the *umiaq* and the general cleaning and refurbishment described in the ethnohistoric sources are consistent with the treatment of the *umiaq* as an animate 'object-being', comparable to Melanesian canoes. Like the new boots and parkas of the human crew, the *umiaq* was clothed in new skins, cleansed and renewed for the whaling season. Just as whales were attracted to cleanliness, new clothing and well-maintained implements, they sought *umiat* that appeared bright and new (Crowell 2009b, 208). The awakening rites and the rites of renewal may be considered rites of passage that readied both the human crew and the *umiaq* itself for whaling. Whaling was – and remains today – a high-risk proposition with success dependent upon many factors, only some of which are under human control. For 19th-century Inupiat and Yupiit, a successful whaling season ensured enough food for the year. Failure signalled not just hunger but also a breach in human–animal relations. Human carelessness or misbehaviour was a common cause of such breaches. Rites of passage thus functioned to ready participants for the physical rigours and ritual demands of whaling season. Lantis (1938, 450), who compiled a set of cross-cultural characteristics of whaling societies, wrote that the complex of rites associated with whaling mark 'the solemnity, the precautions, and the honor accorded the profession of whaling and the men who successfully practiced it'. The evidence discussed in this chapter indicates that not just humans but also the *umiaq* and the materials used to construct it were participants in and recipients of those solemnities, precautions and honour. Along with the use of special boat amulets, the practice of rites of passage bolsters the argument that the *umiaq* was an agent acting cooperatively with the crew, deploying its own assemblage of materials and affordances in pursuit of prey.

The umiaq as agent

In contrast to Torres Strait canoes, there appears to be no evidence of the *umiaq* as a predator. Rather, the *umiaq*, its amulets and crew appear to have exerted an attractive force upon prey. Whales were drawn to the clean, bright cover of the *umiaq*, to the *umialiq* whose wife shared food generously, and to crews who spoke properly and respectfully of prey. So, while Melanesian canoes and Western Arctic *umiat* appear to share agency, that agency differed in its expression. While there are elements of predation evident in whaling practice (the formal analogy between the whaling harpoon and the amulet featuring a shorebird beak, for example), the *umiaq* itself does not appear to be the vehicle for this symbolism, as in Torres Strait (McNiven 2018). The *umialiq* and his wife reportedly provided the boat with food and drink and McNiven's description of canoes as predators suggests a similar need to consume. However, voraciousness and uncontrolled consumption were strongly discouraged among Inupiat and Yupiit. Feeding the *umiaq* was more likely an example of food sharing, a highly valued act of reciprocity consistent with the *umiaq* as kin or collaborator. Food sharing was one way of materialising kin relations, partnerships and mutual assistance agreements. Thus, the provision of food and drink is a rite of social incorporation, marking the *umiaq* as an agent and object-being.

Discussion and conclusions

The idea of the *umiaq* as an 'object-being' broadens the human and animal relational sphere and implicates certain types of 'things' in the social networks that linked humans to the sea and large prey, such as walrus and whales. I have suggested here that certain 'things', such as watercraft and other composite artefacts, assembled of heterogeneous plant and animal materials and transformed through human labour, may be especially good candidates for agency, animation and personhood. In the Arctic, drums and certain types of hunting tools, such as harpoons, appear to have this potential which may have substantial time depth (Grønnow 2012). Whitridge (2004) has already made this argument with regard to harpoons and a key point that he makes is relevant here. That is, harpoons, like watercraft, operate as mediators, 'to physically connect the whalers to the whale, holding fast a relationship that was previously tenuous and subject to the vagaries of wind and tide' (Whitridge 2004, 462).

The *umiaq* also played a mediating role on several levels (Anichtchenko 2016, 116). As watercraft, it enabled land- and ice-bound humans to enter the marine realm, having mobilized the resiliency and water resistance of seal or walrus skin and the inherent buoyancy of driftwood. In constructing the *umiaq*, these affordances of animals and plants were brought into service of human needs. The *umialiq* and his wife facilitated the material transformation of animal lives and driftwood by sponsoring the labour to construct the *umiaq* frame and sew the skin covering. They, too, acted as mediators in the hunt itself, working with the *umiaq* to attract and please whales, their primary prey.

Umiat as 'object-beings' participated in these complex relational networks that linked whales, whaling crews, and captains. Arguably, the relational network stretched further, to include those who participated in the kin- and marriage-linked system of reciprocity that distributed whale and other resources throughout the human community (Spencer 1972; Ellanna 1988; Burch 2006).

In this chapter, I have suggested that watercraft in the Western Arctic might be productively viewed as assemblages of materials and processes encompassing plants, animals and humans. Through the transformational labour of men and women, and the material affordances of driftwood and sea mammals, a productive, hybrid composite was assembled in the form of the *umiaq*. Gender, kinship, humans, animals and plants are all visible in the construction and deployment of the *umiaq*, which itself was productive of new relations. The *umiaq* made interaction between humans and whales possible. Considering watercraft and other complex artefacts and features as assemblages brings these networks of relations and material transformations into focus. Whitridge (2004, 457) has explored how an Inuit harpoon head may be re-envisioned as part of a relational network – while nominally a technological artefact, a harpoon head may be

> enlisted in all sorts of social roles and settings ... a site of symbolic differentiation, of generational dialogues on craft ... or intersocietal dialogues on social difference and identity. Through variation in the use of raw materials, the harpoon head could be enrolled into material discourses on access to exotic commodities, wealth, and status ... or a cosmological discourse on the proper ritual handling of animal substances.

Drums, closely associated with shamanism in the Arctic, are another category of composite artefact that assembles affordances (animal skin or hide and wood) and mediates between and among humans and other types of entities. Some drums apparently had life cycles that paralleled the lives of their users and were broken upon the shaman's death (Rast and Wolff 2016). Exploring the drum as an assemblage of materials and affordances may implicate the instrument in a much broader network that extends well beyond the shaman, their community and non-human entities. Elsewhere, hoards, barrows and medicine bundles – all potent composites of memory and place – have been considered as assemblages (Hamilakis and Jones 2017). Acts or events, such as a feast, may yield new insights as sensorial or affective assemblages (Hamilakis 2017). In short, assemblage thinking opens new avenues of inquiry to archaeologists and permits us to evaluate familiar objects and artifacts in novel ways. In the Western Arctic, looking at watercraft as an assemblage highlights the 'extended sociality' that characterized Inupiat and Yupiit relations with (some) plants, animals and material culture. As both an 'object-being' and a multi-species assemblage, the *umiaq* was much more than a hunting technology – it was an agent in the dynamic relational networks that comprised 19th-century Inupiaq and Yupik societies.

References

Ainana, L., Tatyga, V., Typykhkak, P. and Zagrebin, I.A. (2003) *Umiak: the traditional skin boat of the coast dwellers of the Chukchi Peninsula*, Trans. R.L. Bland. Anchorage, Shared Beringian Heritage Program, National Park Service.

Alix, C. (2009) Appendix D: artifact descriptions: wood. In P.M. Bowers (ed.) *The Archaeology of Deering, Alaska: final report on the Deering Village Safe Water Archaeological Program*. Appendices, vol. 2, D49–D78. Fairbanks, Northern Land Use Research.

Alix, C. (2016) A critical resource: wood use and technology in the North American Arctic. In T.M. Friesen and O.K. Mason (eds) *The Oxford Handbook of the Prehistoric Arctic*, 109–129. New York, Oxford University Press.

Alix, C., Mason, O.K. and Norman, L.E.Y. (2018) Whales, wood, and baleen in Northwestern Alaska: reflection on whaling through wood and boat technology at the Rising Whale site. In Lee, S.-M. (ed.) *Whale on the Rock II*, 41–68. Ulsan, Korea, Ulsan Petroglyph Museum.

Anichtchenko, E.V. (2016) Open Passage: ethno-archaeology of skin boats and indigenous maritime mobility of North American Arctic, Unpublished Ph.D. dissertation, Centre for Maritime Archaeology, University of Southampton.

Anichtchenko, E.V. (2020) Alaska and Eurasia – divergence and continuity across the Bering Strait. In H. Luukkanen (ed.) *The Bark Canoes and Skin Boats of Northern Eurasia*, 215–231. Washington DC, Smithsonian Books.

Anichtchenko, E.V. and Crowell, A.L. (2010) Baidary tihookcanskikh eskimosov po dannym arkheologii i etnografii/Open skin boats of the Pacific Eskimos according to the archaeological and ethnographic data. In I.E. Berezkin (ed.) *Etnografiia i Arkheologiia Korennogo Naseleniia Ameriki/ Ethnography and Archaeology of the Indigenous Population of America*, 198–227. St Petersburg, Nauka.

Bodenhorn, B. (1990) I'm not the great hunter, my wife is": Iñupiat and anthropological models of gender. *Études/Inuit/Studies* 14 (1/2), 55–74.

Bogojavlensky, S. (1969) Imaangmiut Eskimo Careers: Skinboats in Bering Strait. Unpublished Ph.D. Thesis, Department of Social Relations, Harvard University.

Braund, S.R. (1988) *The Skin Boats of Saint Lawrence Island, Alaska*. Seattle WA, University of Washington Press.

Burch, E.S. (2006) *Social Life in Northwest Alaska: the structure of Iñupiaq Eskimo nations*. Fairbanks, University of Alaska Press.

Collins, H.B. (1927). Archeological Expeditions – Nunivak Island and Bering Sea Region – Field Notes 1927, box 53, Henry B. Collins Collection, National Anthropological Archives, Smithsonian Institution, Washington DC.

Crowell, A.L. (2009a) The art of Iñupiaq whaling: elders' interpretations of International Polar Year ethnological collections. In I. Krupnik, M.A. Lang and S.E. Miller (eds) *Smithsonian at the Poles: contributions to International Polar Year science*, 99–113. Washington DC, Smithsonian Institution Scholarly Press.

Crowell, A.L. (2009b) Sea mammals in art, ceremony, and belief: knowledge shared by Yupik and Iñupiaq elders. In W.W. Fitzhugh, J. Hollowell and A.L. Crowell (eds) *Gifts from the Ancestors: ancient ivories of Bering Strait*, 206–225. Princeton NJ, Princeton University Art Museum.

Curtis, E.S. (1930) *The North American Indian*, vol. 20, *The Alaskan Eskimo*. Norwood MA, Plimpton Press.

Deleuze, G. and Parnet, C. ([1977] 1987) *Dialogues*, Trans. H. Tomlinson and B. Habberjam. New York, Columbia University Press.

Ellanna, L.J. (1988) Skin boats and walrus hunters of Bering Strait. *Arctic Anthropology* 25 (1), 107–19.

Fair, S.W. (2005) The northern umiak: shelter, boundary, identity. In K.A. Breisch and A.K. Hoagland (eds) *Building Environments: perspectives in vernacular architecture*, 233–248. Knoxville TN, University of Tennessee Press.

Fienup-Riordan, A. (1994) *Boundaries and Passages: rule and ritual in Yup'ik Eskimo oral tradition*. Norman OK, University of Oklahoma Press.

Friesen, T.M. (2016) Pan-Arctic population movements: the early Paleo-Inuit and Thule Inuit migrations. In T.M. Friesen and O. K. Mason (eds) *The Oxford Handbook of the Prehistoric Arctic*, 673–691. New York, Oxford University Press.

Grønnow, B. (2012) The backbone of the Saqqaq Culture: a study of the nonmaterial dimensions of the early Arctic small tool tradition. *Arctic Anthropology* 49 (2), 58–71. doi: 10.1353/arc.2012.0024.

Hamilakis, Y. (2017) Sensorial assemblages: affect, memory and temporality in assemblage thinking. *Cambridge Archaeological Journal* 27 (1), 169–182. doi: 10.1017/S0959774316000676.

Hamilakis, Y. and Jones, A.M. (2017) Archaeology and assemblage. *Cambridge Archaeological Journal* 27 (1), 77–84. Doi: 10.1017/S0959774316000688.

Hill, E. (2011) Animals as agents: hunting ritual and relational ontologies in prehistoric Alaska and Chukotka. *Cambridge Archaeological Journal.* 21 (3), 407–426.

Hill, E. (2012) The nonempirical past: enculturated landscapes and other-than-human persons in Southwest Alaska. *Arctic Anthropology.* 49 (2), 41–57.

Hill, E. (2013) Archaeology and animal persons: towards a prehistory of human–animal relations. *Environment and Society: advances in research.* 4, 117–136.

Jensen, A.M. (2012) The material culture of Iñupiat whaling: an ethnographic and ethnohistorical perspective. *Arctic Anthropology* 49 (2), 143–161.

Jervis, B. (2019) *Assemblage Thought and Archaeology. Themes in Archaeology.* London, Routledge.

Kaplan, S. A., Jordan, R.H. and Sheehan, G.W. (1984) An Eskimo whaling outfit from Sledge Island, Alaska. *Expedition* (winter), 16–23.

Lantis, M. (1938) The Alaskan whale cult and its affinities. *American Anthropologist* 40 (3), 438–464.

Lantis, M. (1947) *Alaskan Eskimo Ceremonialism.* New York, J.J. Augustin.

Laugrand, F. and Oosten, J. (2015) *Hunters, Predators and Prey: Inuit perceptions of animals.* New York, Berghahn.

LeMoine, G. and Darwent, C. (2016) Development of Polar Inughuit Culture in the Smith Sound region. In T.M. Friesen and O.K. Mason (eds) *The Oxford Handbook of the Prehistoric Arctic*, 873–896. New York, Oxford University Press.

Lowenstein, T. (1993) *Ancient Land, Sacred Whale: the Inuit hunt and its rituals.* New York, Farrar, Straus, and Giroux.

McNiven, I.J. (2018) Torres Strait canoes as social and predatory object-beings. In E. Harrison-Buck and J.A. Hendon (eds) *Relational Identities and Other-Than-Human Agency in Archaeology*, 167–196. Boulder CO, University Press of Colorado.

Morrow, P. (2002) A woman's vapor: Yupik bodily powers in Southwest Alaska. *Ethnology* 41 (4), 335–348.

Müller, M. (2015) Assemblages and actor-networks: rethinking socio-material power, politics and space. *Geography Compass* 9 (1), 27–41. doi: https://doi.org/10.1111/gec3.12192.

Murdoch, J. (1892) *Ethnological Results of the Point Barrow Expedition.* Washington DC, Government Printing Office.

Nelson, E.W. (1899) *The Eskimo about Bering Strait.* Washington DC, Government Printing Office.

Ostermann, H. and Holtved, E. (1952) *The Alaskan Eskimos as Described in the Posthumous Notes of Dr. Knud Rasmussen*, trans. W.E. Calvert. Copenhagen, Gyldendal.

Petersen, H.C. (1986) *Skinboats of Greenland.* Roskilde, Viking Ship Museum and National Museum of Denmark.

Rainey, F.G. (1947) *The Whale Hunters of Tigara.* New York, Anthropological Papers of the American Museum of Natural History 41.

Rast, T. and Wolff, C.B. (2016) Instruments of change: Late Dorset Palaeoeskimo drums and shamanism on coastal Bylot Island, Nunavut, Canada. *Open Archaeology* 2 (1). doi:10.1515/opar-2016-0004.

Ray, P.H. (1885) Ethnographic sketch of the Natives of Point Barrow. In *Report of the International Polar Expedition to Point Barrow, Alaska*, 37–60. Washington, DC, Smithsonian Institution Press.

Sheehan, G.W. (1985) Whaling as an organizing focus in Northwestern Alaskan Eskimo society. In T.D. Price and J.A. Brown (eds) *Prehistoric Hunter-Gatherers: the emergence of cultural complexity*, 123–154. Orlando FL, Academic Press.

Sheehan, G.W. (1995) Whaling surplus, trade, war and the integration of prehistoric Northern and Northwestern Alaskan economies, A.D. 1200–1826. In A.P. McCartney (ed.) *Hunting the Largest Animals: native whaling in the Western Arctic and Subarctic*, 185–206. Edmonton, Canadian Circumpolar Institute Press.

Silook, P. (1917a) Silook Journals, book X. Daniel S. Neuman Papers, MS 162, box 1, folder 10. Juneau, Historical Collections, Alaska State Library.

Silook, P. (1917b) Silook Journals, book XII. Daniel S. Neuman Papers, MS 162, box 1, folder 11. Juneau, Historical Collections, Alaska State Library.

Silook, P. (1937) Stories & Ceremonies. Paul Silook Papers, MS 276, series 2, journal 3. Juneau, Historical Collections, Alaska State Library.

Spencer, R.F. (1959) *The North Alaskan Eskimo: a study in ecology and society.* Washington DC, Government Printing Office.

Spencer, R.F. (1972) The social composition of the North Alaskan whaling crew. In L. Guemple (ed.) *Alliance in Eskimo Society*, 110–120. Seattle WA, University of Washington Press.

Whitridge, P. (2004) Whales, harpoons, and other actors: Actor-Network Theory and hunter-gatherer archaeology. In G.M. Crothers (ed.) *Hunters and Gatherers in Theory and Archaeology*, 445–474. Carbondale IL, Center for Archaeological Investigations, Southern Illinois University.

Chapter 3

Between realms of being: signs of liminality in ancient Altai stone monuments

Esther Jacobson-Tepfer

Stone memorials from the Bronze Age in the Mongolian Altai Mountains reveal a deep-seated belief in the in-dwelling spirits of mountains, springs and rocks. This animism, as well as related understandings regarding the trajectory of human life, are mirrored in the huge compendium of petroglyphic compositions from that same region and time. The rock art reveals an understanding that life taken, as in a hunt, must be replenished. The source of that replenishment is a female figure who functions, also, as the guardian of the roads that lead to the land of the dead. Slender horses, with or without chariots, were understood as the means by which the dead made that last journey. From this mythic conception, together with that preserved in the monumental archaeology, there emerges an understanding of the essential liminality between the natural world and human mythic space.

Animism in ancient religions was the organising principle for the collected papers of the CAMNES 2021 symposium that is the basis of this volume. In developing this subject from the original presentation into a written form, I am struck by how elusive that concept is in the case of prehistoric religion. It might be possible, even reasonable, to expect the existence of in-dwelling spirits within ancient religious systems; but if there is no documentation other than non-verbal material artefacts of that ancient culture – no written texts from within or outside the society in question – certainty remains out of reach. On the other hand, those non-verbal artefacts may point to an aspect of ancient belief that is akin to animism, and that is the concept of liminality.

Derived from the word *limen*, Latin for threshold, liminality refers to the passage in space or time between states of being or that which divides what went before from that which comes after. In psychology, liminal refers to a point beyond which sensation becomes too faint to be experienced. In cultural anthropology, it refers to a 'transitional or intermediate state between culturally defined stages of a person's life' (OED). In its reference to change, the term is most typically used to refer to rites of passage, such as birth, marriage and death (Van Gennep 1909, Wiseman 2019). With reference to the concrete memorial structures of prehistory, such as stone mounds, standing stones or altars, liminality may refer to the idea of passage from this world to the next. In the context of a prehistoric pictorial record, such as that of petroglyphic rock art, the term may also refer to the elusive place where the human becomes intertwined or fused with the non-human. In this respect, the concept of liminality may be expanded from traditionally understood rites of passage to include the substances or forms of being through which those rites carry us. In that regard, the concept opens the way to thinking of boundaries dividing human and non-human, living and dead, as porous and impermanent.

The temporal frame of my paper is the Bronze Age of northern Asia, usually dated from the late 3rd down to the early 1st millennium BCE. The physical context is the northern Altai range. These mountains rise in present-day Russian Altai Republic and continue down to the southeast through a long swarth of western Mongolia, to settle into the Gobi Desert. Along the way the range defines the boundary between Mongolia and the Altai Republic and between Mongolia and China's Xinjiang Province. To the north, the Altai merge into the Sayan Mountains of western Tuvy. These conjoined uplifts at the heart of Eurasia influence the character of land to the west and east. They essentially block the moisture carried by South Asian Westerlies so that the western side of the mountains is well forested, while the Mongolian side is relatively dry and rocky, far less inviting for human habitation. On the other hand, the great glaciers that once draped those mountains carved out long valleys leading down from the ridges into the grassy steppe on the east.[1] These valleys provided the routes by which ancient hunters and fishers and, later, pastoralists moved up into the high country in the Bronze Age, seeking good hunting grounds and rich pastureland. During the Bronze Age, Altai society and systems of belief seem to have been more closely tied to those of the taiga of south Siberia than to the dry lands of present-day Central Asia and north China.[2]

In the present, the Altai landscape may be described as dry mountain steppe with a climate that is extremely cold and windy throughout much of the year. In the Bronze Age, however, the mountains were more forested and the valleys offered richer riparian zones. The animal world was consequently very different from that of today. When we began the Mongolian portion of our project, we could still see wolves and snow leopards, argali and ibex; and golden eagles, cinereous vultures and lammergeyer wheeled above us as we moved over the slopes. Working in the high valleys, we frequently observed the huge vultures and lammergeyers stripping the bodies of dead animals of their flesh and, in so doing, cleaning the land as they have done for thousands of years. Now, however, much of that wildlife has disappeared, negatively impacted by humans, their flocks and climate change.

Retrieving the structures of prehistoric belief systems is an exercise in imaginative thinking. I do not mean to say that we can or should create out of whole cloth belief systems from a distant past. That has been frequently tried but with dubious results. Rather, I would assert that informed imagination is sometimes the only way we can begin to detect the obscure traces of beliefs that disappeared long ago. By that expression I refer to a willingness to observe the recurrence of signifying structures in the material world, to consider those structures within a culturally comparative basis and to follow those traces to careful hypotheses regarding the shape of ancient belief. Here I use the phrase, signifying structures, in a very particular manner. I wish to refer to the character of the repeated relationships between material signs, or the way they are related. These repeated formulations qualify as signs in themselves; when located within a larger, geophysical setting, they become even more resonant with meaning. I realize that the approach I describe here is a bit abstract but hopefully it will become clearer during the following discussion.

Despite the cold and wind that grips the Altai region, within the high valleys are many signs of an ancient human presence. They are found in a rich variety of stone monuments that dot the landscape, sometimes in considerable numbers. They appear, also, in thousands of rock-pecked images found covering mountain bedrock and boulders (Jacobson-Tepfer 2015; 2019). This material provides a *de facto* pictorial text by which we can begin to read life back into the high valleys. The rock art and surface structures together reflect the presence of ancient populations, their lives and deaths and the tenacity of their beliefs relating to death and the passage to another realm. And while the monumental typologies are quite different one from the other, they share implications of a certain cosmic order.

Although my focus here will be petroglyphic rock art, the traces of belief systems found in surface monuments are also relevant, especially those that date from the Bronze Age. It may be best to begin there but with a modern version and work back. There is one monument type known in the present that hints at meaning latent in more ancient stones and reveals certain persistent relationships between humans and their land. The structure I refer to is called an oboo or ovoo. Oboo are piles of stone visible on high ridges, at passes or at the sides of springs.[3] In many cases they appear to have been raised around ancient standing stones or they may even be a continuation into the modern period of ancient stone mounds. Whatever their form, oboo are understood in the present to mark the locus of indwelling spirits and as such are accorded respect and reverence by those who pass by. Such travellers typically circum-ambulate the oboo in a clockwise fashion while adding a stone to the existing pile. They may also leave branches and strips of cloth, as well as offering a libation of tea, yak milk or alcoholic beverage. Rising from the earth into the sky and decorated with the branches of trees, the oboo may be understood as a metaphor for the World Mountain or for the Cosmic Tree. As such, the structure type refers to the concept of passage from one world to another. It points to a generalized animism still found in this part of the world: to a belief that there are spirits immanent in the material forms of the natural world. In the way the oboo refers to a mountain or a tree, it becomes a metaphor for the concept of liminality.

As a monument type, oboo have an ancient ancestor dating back to the Bronze Age. This is a massive standing stone, either solitary or raised in groups of two, three or even four (Fig. 3.1). These stones are usually undecorated but their individualized tonalities and textures suggest that whoever erected them did so with an aesthetic concern as well as with a functional purpose. Originally these standing stones were framed at their bases by rectangular frames and they would be embellished by three or more circular altars on their east side. These two elements have frequently been so trampled by animals over time that they are disrupted or lost. Order and directionality appear to have been a fundamental part of the significance of the standing stone. Where there is only one stone, it stands with its wide sides to the east and west. Where there are two or more, they are arranged from north to south. Together with the altars on the east, the stones describe a central pivot within the four quarters; and within that cosmic diagram, the east – the direction associated in that part of the world with warmth and life – is of paramount importance. Furthering the resonance of this monument type, the stone itself is always what we call mountain stone: hewn from a cliff or brought down by a glacier from higher elevations. The circular altars are always river stones: cobbles that have been smoothed and rubbed by running water. As an integrated setting in space, the standing stone thus serves as a metaphor

Fig. 3.1: *Standing stones in intact frame. Height ca. 1.5 m. The circular altars on the east are broken. View to southwest. Chigirtein Nuur, Sagsay sum.*

for cosmic order. In that respect it is an earlier and richer model of the oboo. The massive standing stone points to a liminal place where physical matter gives way to the immaterial structures of belief.

In this mountainous region of North Asia there is neither continuous memory nor written texts to recapture the ancient beliefs. There is, however, a vast visual text. I refer here to the pecked imagery covering outcrops and boulders within several high valleys. This pictorial material is all petroglyphic; if any was ever painted, the coloration has long since disappeared. The surfaces or panels with imagery are not visible to the casual passer-by. One seeks them by leaving low-lying paths and climbing the slopes where most people do not bother to go. The location of this rock art reflects the trajectories of Bronze Age hunters in search of game and of herders who moved slowly, by foot, up the mountains with their flocks, stopping to find temporary shelter for themselves and their animals on protective terraces. As they moved or during their sojourns, they would decorate the outcrops and boulders along their way. While time and the elements have impacted the surviving rock art, the remote character of this region means that there has been relatively little anthropogenic destruction.

For those who find the panels of rock art dating to the Bronze Age, their representations appear to be rooted in the phenomenal world – pictorial replications of everyday activities and of the inhabitants of their world. The pecked compositions include images of wild and domesticated animals, seen individually and in groups, as well as scenes of hunters and herders. Far fewer in number are scenes of conflict; these perhaps reflect contested control of desired pastures or hunting grounds. Human figures are overwhelmingly male in gender but, as we will see, the appearance of females is important. The styles in which these panels are executed are thoroughly naturalistic. They reflect generations of artists who looked at the world around them with a keen sense of physical reality but they also indicate a fine ability to evoke the personalities of animal types and the details of hair, legs, feet and heads.

For years, as I located and recorded the panels of imagery covering the slopes adjoining rivers, I was impressed by how the pictorial material seemed bound to the real, lived world. One might almost say that, in comparison with other major rock art traditions, that of the Altai was very earth-bound. There were, however, several elements that gave me pause. One was the curious persistence of a birthing woman motif; a second was the appearance of a strange, faceless and horned being. Others included female figures in unexpected contexts, paired horses and images of what looked like winter dwellings, with entrances, a central hearth and interior rooms. Within a pictorial tradition so resolutely bound to the phenomenal world, the strangest aspect was the total absence of any signs of death. True, there are many scenes of elk or horses or ibex being attacked by predators but never are these prey animals even pulled down. For all the images of conflict, also, there are never any representations of human death. With time, I realized that these characteristics of the rock art tradition demanded an approach that was both released from attachment to the phenomenal reference and highly integrative.

In this inquiry, perhaps the most fundamental motif to be considered is that of the birthing woman. This image appears among the most ancient motifs in the Mongolian Altai, noticeably alongside massive aurochs, archaic horses and even rhinoceros. The earliest examples, from a site known as Aral Tolgoi, have the worn and rough-pecked appearance of imagery from the late Palaeolithic period (13,000–11,000 cal BP). The figures are frontal, legs bent up at the knees in a birthing position. Ungainly and certainly very old, they attest to an ancient concern with fecundity and the giving of life.[4]

From that period and into the early Holocene (ca. 10,500 cal BP) come the earliest scenes of hunting, the animals massive and the hunters small and awkward at best. One might say that the juxtaposed animals and human figures were signs of a hunt but gave no sense of its psychological significance. Thereafter and for perhaps 5000 years, imagery essentially disappeared from known rock art sites of the Altai. This huge lacuna probably refers to a time when people did not move into the high mountains: the upper valleys were still glacier choked and the slopes were becoming too heavily forested to serve as habitat for traditional hunting prey such as aurochs and wild horses. However, beginning about 4500 years ago, forests began to retreat, lake levels to fall and climate became cooler and drier. Presumably it was in the succeeding centuries that rock art began to re-appear in the high mountains, the pecked imagery tracing the return of hunters and later herders.

This period, which we can date to the late fourth millennium BCE, coincides with the beginning of the Bronze Age in this part of North Asia. The animals represented continued to be massive and relatively static profile figures but now pecked out entirely in silhouetted forms and sometimes seen in groups, suggesting the herds that had re-appeared in the valleys. It was also at that time that representations of hunters began to combine with animals but, while the animal imagery was executed in profile forms, the humans were at first executed frontally, brandishing crude weaponry such as clubs or a kind of bow. There are few such compositions, but one from the Baga Oigor complex is significant. In this case, the images of a frontal hunter and his prey, a large horned animal, were executed beside much earlier images of two birthing women.[5] In a world where there was no lack of stone surfaces, the artist's decision to peck his hunting scene alongside primitive birthing figures was certainly meaningful, as if the artist wished to draw some aspect of her power into his hunting.

That deliberate juxtaposition appears again in a much later panel from the same complex. Within a composition laid out over several boulders appear three profile archers and a mass of wild animals. On the side of the largest boulder are two frontal birthing women, surrounded by animals.[6] Covered by the images of wild animals, birthing women and hunters, the boulders were transformed by the artist into the slopes of a mountain on which is detailed an essential relationship between female fecundity and the success of the hunt. This connection between birthing women and hunting scenes echoes the observations of several ethnographers who have pointed to archaic traditions in the Altai and Sayan regions preserved to the present. In these, the spirit of a mountain was understood to be female, a protector and generator of game. Her favour was essential for the success of a hunt and for the return of new game to the mountain (Kyzlasov 1982). In these cases, the female represents a place of transition from non-being to being; she allows the taking of animals by the hunter but then replenishes them.

The motif of the birthing woman continued to appear in a variety of forms throughout the Bronze Age, but one strange variation deserves mention since it points to liminality on several levels. This is an image that is best described as a horned, faceless, bell-shaped figure.[7] These figures usually lack arms but sometimes have legs. Several are approached by large animals; in some cases, small animals appear within the strange horned images, as if to refer to their female, generative character. The most descriptive of these images is within a panel in TS V in the Baga Oigor complex (Fig. 3.2). Here the horned figure combines a human body with an outer bell frame and she (for the image is clearly female in gender) is shown giving birth to a human child. This remarkable figure is approached on her right by several large animals. The panel looks out over Baga Oigor Gol (river) and beyond that to the snow-crested ridge of Taldagiin Ikh Uul (mountain). Like several other images of

Fig. 3.2: *Detail of a larger panel: birthing spirit figure on the right approaching animals on the left. Bronze Age. TS V, Baga Oigor complex.*

bell-shaped figures, with or without interior figures, this panel can be dated to the full Bronze Age (mid-2nd millennium BCE).

The understanding of this strange figure type is controversial. Some scholars have interpreted it as a shaman (*e.g.*, Kubarev 2002) but, aside from its quasi-human appearance, there is no basis for such an understanding. I prefer to refer to it simply as a spirit figure. Given its human/non-human character, its facelessness combined with signs of fecundity, it is clearly a figure that points to the liminal space of creation. We cannot be certain that the orientation of the panel to both the river and the mountain is deliberate but we can say that a similar orientation pertains to several other faceless figures in the Baga Oigor complex and suggests that the river and possibly the mountain expand the figure's significance, suggesting a route to another realm. However, not all these figures are so oriented. Several appear either on a rock wall, like a featureless window into another world and one remarkable image has been pecked into a flat paving stone, almost invisible in the ground.[8] These last images suggest another aspect of the spirit figure: its existence between an outer world and an inner one, as if existing at the door to a passage into another realm.

Birthing women do not disappear from rock art until late in the Bronze Age but women identified by long gowns and hair begin to appear more frequently in scenes of the later Bronze Age. The image of a woman becomes especially common with the appearance of scenes of families caravanning with loaded yaks and horses into the high pastures. The appearance of such an image reflects the practice of transhumance that emerged by the middle of the 2nd millennium BCE, when herders began to move into high mountain pastures for the summer months. The massive yaks carrying the family's goods are frequently shown carrying the family's collapsed portable dwelling, known as a ger (or yurt). As if that were not enough, their load is often topped with the children of the household or with an old person. In most cases, a woman is seen at the head of the caravan, often holding the lead rope to the first loaded yak (Fig. 3.3). Of course, this motif may be nothing more than a statement of fact: that in real life women would be leading the packed animals while the men walk at the side, bows ready, as if prepared for an attack on the caravan of for an opportunistic hunt. The frequency with which the woman appears with the family caravan suggests that she had become a sign of family well-being, just as the yaks loaded with children and furnishings represented the home as the centre of the family. We can say that the loaded yak represents the family household and its wellbeing, while the animals and the motif of the hunt re-affirm the household's dependency on a wilder world. The composition is thus both a reflection of reality, an evocation of the integration of human and non-human worlds within the potent space of the mountain, and an indication of the centrality of the female to that balance.

A more intriguing motif, however, is that of a woman standing by a hunter or within the precincts of the hunt. This is vividly represented by a large panel from the Tsagaan Gol complex, in which a tall woman (recognizable as such by her long gown), stands at the side of a hunting scene centred by a large elk.[9] All around the elk are small archers attacking that animal and others and the whole scene is filled

Fig. 3.3: Scene with loaded yak led by a woman and accompanied by animals and hunters. Late Bronze Age. Upper Tsagaan Gol complex.

with the visual cacophony of dogs and fleeing caprids. This curious placement of a woman within the scene of a hunt is not unique. An especially beautiful instance occurs in a panel from the Baga Oigor complex (Fig. 3.4a). Here a woman, so identified by her long gown and hair, stands behind an archer who is aiming his bow intently on the aurochs before him.[10] In this case, again, the basic juxtaposition is unlikely: one would hardly expect to find a woman following a hunt, especially without any visible weapon. The motif must rather be a variation on the theme of the woman as a sign of fecundity and the mistress of the mountain as the means by which the hunter's game is replenished. The woman is again a sign of the threshold between the world of the living and the spirit realm, the source of new game.

There are several variations on the motif of the hunter and the woman as a sign of fecundity. One seems to refer to an ancient Altai tradition according to which, on the eve of his hunt the hunter should sleep on the mountain where he will make love to its mistress, and that this will ensure not only the success of his hunt but also the replenishment of game. This theme is reflected in panels where we find images of what are euphemistically referred to as loving couples juxtaposed with scenes of the hunt itself, or with a view of the hunter. In one superb example from the upper Tsagaan Gol complex, hunters bracket two magnificent Red Deer while below can be seen a couple in embrace.[11] Just as it is highly unlikely that women would appear in the middle of a hunting scene, one would not expect to find scenes of copulating

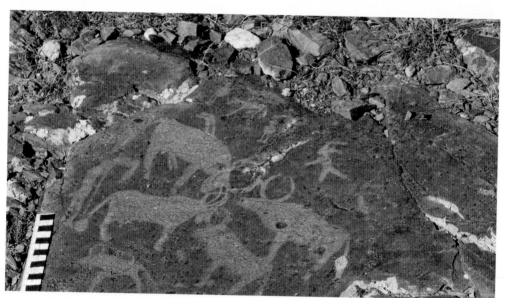

Fig. 3.4: a) Aurochs hunt. In the lower left section is a frontal woman standing beside a profile archer. Late Bronze Age. BO III, Baga Oigor complex; b) detail with two birdmen and two addorsed horses at the top of the panel.

couples within the real world of the hunt. Rather, it seems that all these panels, with their variations on the motif of the female presence, reflect a structure of meaning within which the success of the hunt depended upon signs of regeneration. In these compositions, the narrative bridges two worlds: that of the hunter and that of the mistress of the mountain and her animals. What appears to be a scene taken from everyday life instead refers to the transitional character of human/animal life, of its essential liminality.

In addition to the ger, Bronze Age herders apparently lived in small, sturdy dwellings known today as winter dwellings. Images of these structures appear regularly within petroglyphs of the late Bronze Age. Most often, small female figures appear within their interiors. In some cases, large animals appear near the dwelling, attached to it by long lines as if to indicate the well-being of the household.[12] In other cases, the image of a dwelling complicates the meaning of the composition and works with other elements to suggest a space suspended between this world and the next. For example, on a terrace in BO II, stands a huge boulder covered with images and oriented the Baga Oigor river and distant, snow crested mountains (Fig. 3.5). Most of the south face of the boulder is covered with small, bounding animals stalked by hunters.

These lively images transform the surface into a mountain landscape. At the top of the boulder, on the right, can be seen the outlines of a dwelling, complete with interior

Fig. 3.5: 'Birthing women' rock. Late Bronze Age. BO I, Baga Oigor complex.

rooms, a central hearth, and an entrance on the east side. If we read the dwelling as 'real' then we could conclude it was intended as part of an actual landscape, perhaps even the hunters' dwelling. However, in the upper left of the boulder is another section that redirects the sense of the scene. Six large elk are stretched out in profile, and beside them are three birthing figures, one seemingly touching a doe at her neck. These birthing figures must be the incarnation of the mistress of the mountain; and with their animals, the elk, they represent the regeneration of game. But where does this happen? In this realm or another? The composition seems to balance between two worlds, the land of the living – the hunt, the dwelling – and another realm, that of regeneration.

This curious panel is clarified by the correspondence between the dwelling in the upper right of the panel and a kind of surface monument dated also to the later Bronze Age. These monuments take the form of stone settings laid out directly on the earth. Oriented from east to west, they trace out the designs of true dwellings – with entrances, insulated walls, interior divisions and – most importantly – a hearth. One major difference between these settings and a real winter dwelling is that in addition to an entrance on the east, there is an exit on the west. In certain valleys we have found stone settings by the dozens; and although some scholars have theorized that they are the remains of actual structures, that could not be the case. They are always found on terraces completely unprotected from the cold winds that sweep down from the mountains throughout the year.[13] The few such settings that have been excavated have revealed burnt sacrificial materials in the virtual hearth but nothing of burials. These facts have led me to believe that the stone settings are virtual dwellings, laid out to memorialize a person's death and to project his or her dwelling into the next world.

Certain elements associated with the virtual dwellings make clearer their reference to the next world. These are stone lines that extend from the settings across the plain and either up to a ridge or down to an adjacent river. In one case, from a site called Tsagaan Asgat, a large grouping of virtual dwellings is connected by a long line of cobbles extending up an adjacent slope for about 50 m to end at a large oboo that overlooks the whole valley, the river below and snow-crested mountains to the south. On the nearby terrace of Akh Töbei, where it is possible to see more than 70 dwellings, one long stone line extends across the terrace toward the sacred mountain Tsengel' Khairkhan; another stone line extends down the slope toward the river Tsagaatiin Gol. Here and elsewhere, where we were able to find the stone lines, they seem to trace out a path or road that the deceased person would take to arrive at realm of the dead or of the ancestors. The stone lines affirm the liminal character of the virtual dwellings; and when the virtual dwellings appear in rock art panels – as in that of BO II – they confirm the probability that the hunt, the birthing women, and the dwelling all converge to indicate the liminal character of the scene. The question, of course, is where the body was deposed. I will return to that a little later.

Decades of Russian and Soviet ethnographic research in the northern Altai and Sayan mountains have produced a rich record of Siberian mythic traditions.[14]

These traditions are difficult to deal with: their very antiquity would indicate significant change from the original form, and that change would be heightened by the dispersal of groups out from their native lands. However, throughout the rock art of our area it is possible to find images and combinations of images the reflect several ancient Siberian myths in which appears an originating female source, sometimes glimpsed as part human/part animal. This motif is most vividly reflected in the Evenk myth of a female antlered animal from whose head emerges the tree of life; and in that tree the great birds build their nests and feed the next generation of living beings (Anisimov 1958; 1963). In the Baga Oigor complex we have found at least two rock art panels that appear to reflect that mythic tradition.

Across a large boulder in BO I are spread small scenes of wild animals and hunters, each within a space seemingly carved out by a winding trail (Fig. 3.6). The hunters stand on or beside the tendril-like trail, raising their readied bows towards their prey. The whole scene appears to express the abundance of life on the mountain. In the lower section of the panel, on the right side, is visible a yak loaded with the belongings of a family. This vignette adds to the sense that the boulder forms a real landscape through which the family is moving to new pasture. But there is one other significant element. To the right of the family group and along the lower edge of the boulder a small deer has been inserted. From its antlers sprout long tendrils that become the paths leading across the mountain landscape. The deer, then, is the origin of the mountain's game and thus the source of its bounty. The mountain, the caravan as a sign for the family threshold, and the deer as generator of all life become integrated into a visual metaphor for the passage between this world and the next. In so doing,

Fig. 3.6: Antler landscape. Bronze Age. BO I, Baga Oigor complex.

the panel points to the liminal nature of life, between land and animals, humans and animals, beginnings (the stag with tendril-like antlers) and ends (the hunt).

Two related motifs found in late Bronze Age rock art also function on the dual levels of phenomenal reality and metaphor. Both point to the cultural understanding of a liminal space between realms of being. The first is the image of a two-wheeled vehicle but these vehicles are curious: sometimes the wheels are spoked, indicating a light vehicle intended for speed and sometimes the wheels are solid, indicating what should be a heavier cart for transporting loads (Jacobson-Tepfer 2012).[15] The horses pulling both kinds of vehicles are sometimes static in their positions and sometimes represented as swift animals, as if pulling the vehicle at great speed. The fact that these vehicles existed in the Altai in the late Bronze Age is believable. They had to have come into North Asia by the later 2nd millennium BCE, most likely brought with migrating herders from Western Siberia.[16] Nonetheless, their appearance here in the high Altai valleys is puzzling. This landscape is uneven steppe covered with cobbles, cobble and boulder strewn slopes and sudden marshlands. While it is possible to understand a slow, heavy vehicle being used for carrying loads in this land it is impossible to imagine a light wooden vehicle bouncing rapidly over the ground without falling apart.[17]

The second but related motif is that of the horse itself. In fact, within the northern Altai, images of horses first appear in the late Palaeolithic, but at that time and throughout the following early and middle Holocene, these animals are of the Przewalski type. Their representations in rock art belong to the same impulse to represent the surrounding world as is revealed in images of other large animals such as elk, aurochs, and ibex. In the late Bronze Age, and certainly by the later 2nd millennium BCE, another kind of horse makes its appearance. It may be represented individually or in small groups but more often the horse is seen in the context of images of wheeled vehicles. This animal, a much more gracile creature than those identified as the Mongolian wild horse (takhi), is believed to have originated in Kazakhstan. That is the type seen in rock art in connection with the so-called chariots and carts. The point that is relevant to this discussion, however, is that in the same period – late 2nd millennium BCE – we find the appearance of a new monument type, known as khirgisuur.[18] The khirgisuur were clearly funerary in purpose, even if they rarely include burials but associated with them are circles presumed to have had a sacrificial function in which horses were the primary animal of sacrifice. These would seem to indicate that whichever social group brought the khirgisuur monument to the Altai, they also brought a tradition in which the sacrifice of horses was necessarily related to death.[19]

There are more than a few aspects of the wheeled vehicle and horse imagery of the Bronze Age that are puzzling. For example, many of the vehicles are driven by archers aiming at a wild animal without holding any reins; or stranger yet, there are no drivers, or no wheels, or no horses or the figure in the basket appears to be dead. In other words, a principle of *pars pro toto* seems to have applied to the representation of the wheeled vehicle (Jacobson-Tepfer 2012); such a principle never applies to other objects, such as human figures or any animals. This supports the argument that many of the visual references to vehicles refer to a mythic rather than real function. Even more curious, within the mountainous region, chariot images frequently appear on high outcrops, far from any feasible track. At the same time, there have been no finds of actual vehicles or their parts within the archaeology of the Altai before the early Iron Age.[20] Taking a clue from burial practices in the mountainous regions of Mongolia over the last few hundred years, one may conclude that the image of the vehicle, whether drawn by horses or not, functioned primarily as a sign of the transportation of a deceased person's body into the mountains for a sky burial or as a sign of the deceased's journey to the next world. Thus, as represented in rock art, the two-wheeled vehicle was a virtual chariot. Like the virtual dwelling, the vehicle referred to the rite of passage from this realm to the next; that is, to a liminal space joining realms of being. Similarly, one may surmise that the horses alone, with or without vehicles, and as represented in sacrificial altars, were understood as the steeds needed to carry the dead to the next realm.

Within rock art of the same period horses may be represented as slender, singular animals or as paired, addorsed horses, as if they were harnessed to a vehicle. In both cases, they may function alone, without the vehicles, as references to the rites of passage attendant on death. This process of simplification of metaphoric imagery and its signification may be seen in several finely pecked panels on a high outcrop in BO III. By subject, style, and manner of execution, these panels were all seemingly done by the same hand. In one scene on the outcrop (Fig. 3.7), a figure is visible in the upper left side of the composition within a squared enclosure. He holds the leads to two addorsed horses, arranged precisely as if they were hitched to a vehicle.[21] Outside, to the right, stands a

Fig. 3.7: Scene from Picture Rock. Late Bronze Age. BO III, Baga Oigor complex.

frontal woman, like a guardian figure, and four other figures, three of whom each lead a single horse. One of these figures and another diminutive one have the bodies and legs of birds, while the figure in the lower section has the horns and tail of an animal.

Close by this curious panel are two other, similar compositions (Fig. 3.8).[22] In the upper scene, another figure crouching within an enclosure holds the leads of two horses, similarly arranged as if hitched to a vehicle. Outside the entrance to the enclosure is a large figure; her thickness and frontal posture indicate that she is a woman. Approaching her from the left is a birdman leading two addorsed horses and followed by two other birdmen.

The lower scene is less complicated. Three birdmen moving right lead two single horses toward an enclosure in which a large female figure with long hair and dress

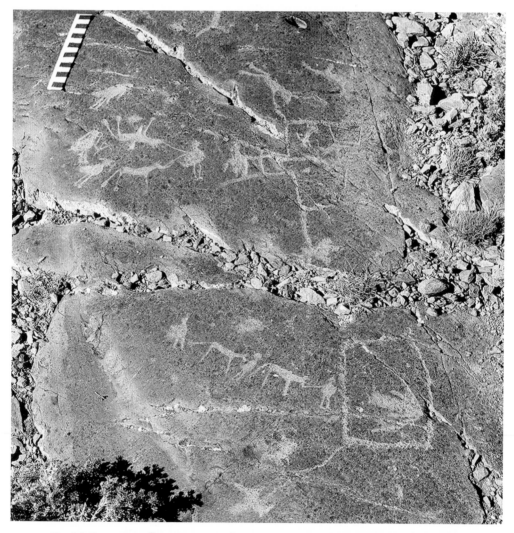

Fig. 3.8: Two scenes from Picture Rock. Late Bronze Age. BO III, Baga Oigor complex.

stands as if in welcome or as if guarding the defined space. In this scene we see no crouched figure but the birdmen and slender horses heading for the enclosure repeat motifs seen in the other images. The execution of these compositions is distinctive; it indicates they were pecked out by the artist who did the scene of an aurochs hunt on the same outcrop. In that scene (Fig. 3.4a, above), a young woman stands beside the archer as if somehow associated with the hunt. At the very top of that boulder and almost invisible, are two birdmen with a pair of horses arranged as if to pull a vehicle (Fig. 3.4b). As in the case of the other compositions on this outcrop, the bird men with horses must refer to the journey to the land of the dead. Together with the woman beside the archer, they refer to a liminal space and experience.

There is one other composition adjacent to the outcrop in BO III with the images just discussed. Style and subject indicate that this panel, also, must have been executed by the same artist (Fig. 3.9).[23] A triangular outcrop is covered with images of wild animals: horses, stags, ibex, wild boar and strutting cranes. The panel is divided in half by a deep, horizontal cleft, but the images on both sides of that break create a vision of a world of abundance. Just above the cleft in the centre, is a caravan scene:

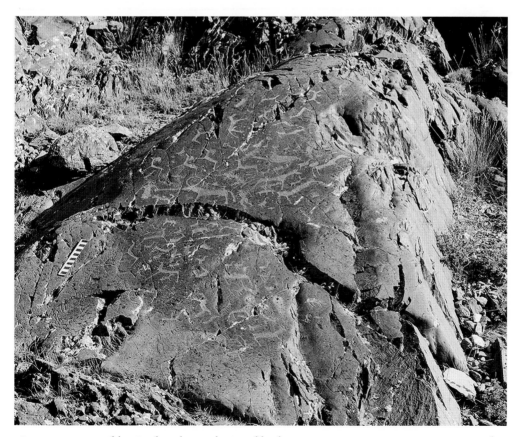

Fig. 3.9: Caravan, wild animal, and spread-winged birds. Late Bronze Age. BO III, Baga Oigor complex.

a woman leads a yak carrying the frame of a yurt and a child, and behind walks a man. On the left edge of the panel (Fig. 3.10) are two vehicles with horses and a small girl. In both sections, we see this world through the wings of large birds in flight or as if from below, looking up at the spread-wings of the huge birds. The motif of large spread-winged birds is not unique in late Bronze Age rock art, but here it is executed with an unusually fine, even elegant, technique.

The woman, the man and the loaded yak carry the motif of the threshold, the centre of a good life and the animals re-affirm a realm of wellbeing. There are no visible signs of sickness or death but the vehicles introduce a note of disquiet. And while the animals and strutting birds conjure a world of abundance through which moves the

Fig. 3.10: Detail of panel in Fig. 3.9, showing great spread-winged birds, wild animals and a chariot with two hitched horses in the lower left. Not visible in this detail is second chariot and a young girl.

small household, the birds in flight unsettle our space and perspective and challenge our location in space: are we above or below? Or perhaps it is impossible to know.

By style and details of subject matter we can date these panels from the high outcrop on BO III to the last third of the 2nd millennium BCE. Such a date makes these panels contemporaneous with the monumental khirgisuur and their circular altars with horse-head burials. As indicated earlier, excavated khirgisuur have rarely included actual burials, and within the Altai region there is no record of bodies interred in the khirgisuur mounds. This would indicate that the bodies of the dead were laid to rest somewhere else, perhaps higher on the adjoining slopes. The khirgisuur also date to the period before chamber burials, which did not make their appearance until the 9th century BCE.[24] In other words, until the end of the Bronze Age, funerary structures did not always include human interments; but with the khirgisuur, we see the clear signs of horse sacrifice being part of the burial ritual.

The compositions in Figures 3.7 and 3.8 clarify the narrative attending death in the late Bronze Age: within those compositions, the enclosure is the dwelling of the dead but as it will be experienced in the next world. The crouching figures holding the reins of horses are the dead with the steeds that will take them on their journeys to that realm. The slender bodies of the horses and, most particularly, their addorsed positions indicate that they are the sign of the chariot we see in so many other compositions. The birdmen with horses, both singular and paired, indicate that they are the signs of the journey after death. The women standing in or just outside the enclosures are the guardians of the road to the land of the dead. In earlier panels these females were represented as the sources of new life, either as birthing women or as women at a hunt. But then, as throughout most of human history, new life was inextricably joined to death. As in a hunt (*e.g.*, Figs 3.4, 3.5), the taking of an animal (death) necessitated its replenishment (life).

The panels discussed above recreate a liminal space within which beings shift from human to animal, and where the spirits of the living take flight to another realm. This is most expressively reflected in the composition on the triangular surface (Figs 3.9, 3.10). Here, where the scene seems to celebrate life, the appearance of the chariots at the side of the composition suggests the journey to another realm. Most unsettling, however, are the great winged birds that veil a large section of the lower surface. These are not the cranes or ducks or other water birds that strut across parts of the composition. These are rather the images of large birds, such as the cinereous vultures or lammergeyers that circle over the steppes and cliffs of this region. In real life and in this composition, these birds are the signs of sky burials, in which the dead would be deposed on high terraces or in the cliffs, and where the large birds would strip the flesh to carry it back to nourish their young. The great birds, like the horses, are signs of that liminal space between the living and the not living, between this realm and the next.

Above the outcrop in BO III, with its extraordinary petroglyphic compositions, the rocky ridge rises approximately 100 m into a place of cliffs and niches and passages before the transition to high pasture. When I climbed up into that rocky labyrinth, I was struck by the complexity of spaces within the slope and by the sense of having moved into another world than that represented by the valley floor. Elsewhere I was puzzled by the appearance of strange stone circles on high ridges, marking places that are otherwise empty and too exposed to serve as animal corrals. Thinking about these places, I have come to believe that the dead – whose ancient burials we cannot find – were laid out in these cliffs, perhaps in the very circles I found on the high slopes. The woman represented within or at the entrance of the enclosures was the guardian to the other world. The chariots and the horses refer to the journey that the dead would undertake but the birdmen and large winged birds were the signs of ultimate renewal.

Within the rock art complexes we recorded in northwestern Mongolia the panels discussed above are unusual in their narrativity. They are not, however, unique. There are many other compositions and images that repeat the motifs I have discussed above, whether it be guardian women, chariots, horses or great birds. Taken as a whole, this material indicates that even if there are no written texts that reveal the belief systems of people in the late Bronze Age, we find the pictorial reflections of those beliefs, and in many different formulations. This imagery reflects the belief in a world poised between the living and the dead, where the road to the land of the dead is guarded by a female deity.[25] On one level the journey after death is undertaken with the aid of horses, signalled also by a chariot; on another level, the journey involves the agency of great birds and their young, through which the deceased become re-incarnated in new life.

Notes

1 The highest Altai peaks in both Mongolia and Russia are still crowned with glaciers, but these are melting rapidly under the impact of global climate change. For a good introduction to the physical geography of the region being considered here, see Jacobson-Tepfer *et al.* (2010) and Jacobson-Tepfer (2020).
2 This is because the cultures associated with the northern Altai region during the Bronze Age were believed to have derived from those in the north, in the region of Khakassia. In addition, during the early Iron Age, herding populations in the Altai were pushed out of that region: to the west, to seek better pasture; or to the north, up the Yenisei drainage, to escape the aggressive expansion of other steppe nomadic peoples.
3 For examples of oboo in the region being discussed here, see Monolian Altai Inventory Collection (*MAIC*) at https://oregondigital.org = *MAIC*: OVOO_00003_TG, VIEW_00014_TG, OVOO_00002_TG.
4 *MAIC*: RA_PETR_AT_0068.
5 *MAIC*: RA_PETR_OI_0102.
6 *MAIC*: RA_PETR_OI_0111, PETR_00357_OI.
7 *MAIC*: spirit figures.
8 *MAIC*: PETR_00205_OI, RA_PETR_OI_0275.
9 *MAIC*: RA_PETR_TG_0835.
10 *MAIC*: RA_PETR_OI_0461.
11 Jacobson-Tepfer 2019: 241–242; *MAIC*: RA_PETR_TG_0418, RA_PETR_TG_0421.

12 *MAIC*: RA_PETR_TG_0240.

13 *MAIC*: dwellings.

14 The people in question include the Ket, a now almost disappeared ethnos, and Evenk, as well as Altaitsi. These people were pushed out of the Altai-Sayan zone by the aggressive expansion of other people in the early Iron Age. For myths and sources, see Jacobson-Tepfer (2015, 314–341).

15 *MAIC*: chariots.

16 The North Asian wheeled vehicle is usually traced back to origins in the Sintashta-Petrovka cultures of the Trans-Ural region, dated to the late 3rd–early 2nd millennia BCE (see Kuznetsov 2006; Lindner 2020).

17 Within the archaeological record, there are no indications that these vehicles were made with metal joining pieces or wheel rims, at least not in the Altai-Sayan region.

18 See, *e.g.*, *MAIC*: RNKH_00030_KV, RNKH_00002_DY, RNKH_00009_TG.

19 The appearance of horse-head sacrifices in association with khirgisuur raises several complex questions. There are indications that the khirgisuur monument type emerged in the Altai-Sayan region in the latter second millennium, but to date horse-head burials have not been found in conjunction with the khirgisuur of that region. On the other hand, they have been found in abundance in association with the more complex khirgisuur of the central aimags. See Allard and Erdenebaatar (2005); Gheyle (2009); Makarewicz *et al.* (2018). Horses were not the only animals so sacrificed: the bones of caprids and even cattle have been attested in some khirgisuur complexes in Central Mongolia (Broderick *et al.* 2014).

20 Chariots and their sacrificed horses were found in the royal burials of the Shang dynasty (14th through late 11th centuries BCE). The earliest wheeled vehicle from the Altai region was found in burial no.5 at Pazyryk, in the Russian Altai. This burial is dated by one source to the early 4th century BCE (Zeitseva *et al.* 1998). The whole question of light, wheeled vehicles – *i.e.*, chariots – in the mountainous regions of Mongolia remains problematic; see Jacobson-Tepfer (2012).

21 *MAIC*: RA_PETR_OI_0337.

22 *MAIC*: RA_PETR_OI_0332, RA_PETR_OI_0333.

23 This fine panel is difficult to see except in details. For closer imagery for this panel and the others discussed above from the same outcrop, see Jacobson-Tepfer (2019, 245–252).

24 The earliest known chamber burial is that of Arzhan 1, in eastern Tuvy, dated to the 9th–8th centuries BCE (Gryaznov 1980). From then on, sub-soil chambers became the standard burial structure.

25 I have treated the theme of the woman as the guardian of the road to the dead in several earlier publications (1997; 2015).

References

Allard, F. and Erdenebaatar, D. (2005) Khirigsuurs, ritual and mobility in the Bronze Age of Mongolia. *Antiquity* 79, 1–18.

Anisimov, A.F. (1958) *Religiya evenkov v istoriko-geneticheskom izuchenii i problemy proiskhozhedeniya pervobyntnykh verovaniy*. Moscow-Leningrad, Academy of Sciences.

Anisimov, A.F. (1963) The Shaman's tent of the Evenks and the origin of the shamanistic rite. In H.N. Michael (ed.) *Studies in Siberian Shamanism*, 84–123. Toronto, Arctic Institute of the North, University of Toronto.

Broderick, L.G., Seitsonen, O., Bayarsaikhan, J. and Houle, J.-H. (2016) Lambs to the slaughter: a zooarchaeological investigation of stone circles in Mongolia. *International Journal of Osteoarchaeology* 26, 537–543.

Gheyle, W. (2009) Highlands and Steppes. an analysis of the changing archaeological landscape of the altay mountains from the eneolithic to the ethnographic period. Unpublished PhD. Dissertation. Ghent University.

Gryaznov, M.P. (1980) *Arzhan.* Leningrad, Nauka.

Jacobson-Tepfer, E. (1997) The Bird-Woman, the Birthing Woman, and the Woman of the Animals: a consideration of the female image in petroglyphs of ancient central Asia. *Arts Asiatiques* 52, 37–59.

Jacobson-Tepfer, E. (2012) The image of the wheeled vehicle in the Mongolian Altai: instability and ambiguity. *The Silk Road* 10, 1–28.

Jacobson-Tepfer, E. (2015) *The Hunter, the Stag, and the Mother of Animals.* Oxford, Oxford University Press.

Jacobson-Tepfer, E. (2019) *The Life of Two Valleys in the Bronze Age.* Eugene OR, Luminare Press.

Jacobson-Tepfer, E. (2020) *The Anatomy of Deep Time.* Cambridge: Cambridge Elements in the Environmental Humanities.

Jacobson-Tepfer, E., Meacham, J. and Tepfer, G. (2010) *Archaeology and Landscape in the Mongolian Altai: an atlas.* Redlands CA, ESRI Press.

Kubarev, V.D. (2002) Traces of shamanic motives in the petroglyphs and burial paintings of the Gorno-Altai. In A. Rozwadowski and M.M. Kosko (eds) *Spirits and Stones,* 99–119. Poznan, Instytut Wischodni, Adam Michiewixz University.

Kuznetsov, P.F. (2006) The emergence of Bronze Age chariots in eastern Europe. *Antiquity* 80, 638–645.

Kyzlasov, I.L. (1982) Gora-praroditel'nitsa v fol'klore khakassov. *Sovetskaya etnographiya* 2, 83–92.

Lindner, S. (2020) Chariots in the Eurasian steppe: a Bayesian approach to the emergence of horse-drawn transport in the early second millennium BC. *Antiquity* 94, 361–380.

Makarewicz, C.A., Winter-Schuh, C., Byerly, H., and Houle, J.-L. (2018) Isotopic evidence for ceremonial provisioning of Late Bronze age khirigsuurs with horses from diverse geographic locales. *Quaternary International* 30, 1–12.

Van Gennep, A. (1909) *Les Rites de Passage: etude systématique des rites.* Paris, Emile Nourry.

Wiseman, R. (2019) Getting beyond rites of passage in archaeology. *Current Anthropology* 60 (4), 449–474.

Zaitseva, G.I., Vasiliev, S.S., Marsadolov, L.S., van der Plicht, J., Sementsov, A.A., Dergachev, V.A. and Lebedeva, L.M. (1998) A tree-ring and 14C chronology of the key Sayan-Altai monuments. *Radiocarbon* 40 (1), 571–580.

Chapter 4

In mantic and hostile lands: surveillance and mimesis by divination in the Late Old Babylonian period

Seth Richardson

This paper surveys the evidence for Babylonian divinatory practices of the Late Old Babylonian period (ca. 17th century BCE). This is a period in which liver divination was often used to predict and protect conditions of travel across open territory to shrines, cities, temple, fields and forts - more so than for almost any other purpose. Catalogues of omens from this time also voice this concern for safety and transit in the countryside. This unease is also reflected in administrative texts and state letters concerned with obtaining information about the movement of troops, the location of enemies, and the safety of goods and forts through field intelligence: from scouts, watchguards, and tribal camps. The parallel concerns for surveillance at the mantic and tactical levels identify an epistemic discourse newly focused on non-urban spaces and concerns, where Mesopotamian ritual and religious attention had previously been focused on cities. Divination was functionally part of a systematic and explicit way of knowledge about landscape, managed through interlocking administrative, ritual, and textual practices. This transformation reflected a changing Babylonian social and political world increasingly characterized by non-state actors and non-urban forms of power.*

Introduction

In the early winter of 1671 BC, a scribe in the Babylonian fortress of Dūr-Abiešuḫ ('Fortress-of-King-Abiešuḫ') wrote out a cuneiform account (CUSAS 29 56) making note of two sheep which had been deducted from the flock of a herd manager named Abu-waqar. The sheep were then used for a divinatory procedure either by or for[1] a man named Etel-pī-Marduk. This was neither the first nor last time that Abu-waqar provided sheep for such a purpose: a string of related administrative texts[2] give evidence that he regularly supplied animals for divinatory rituals in this military complex located just north of the city of Nippur, a city then under threat from unnamed 'enemies'.

Little about this tablet looks impressive: it is small (ca. 50 × 60 × 20 mm), unsealed and contains not more than 60 words, only a third of which (ll. 6–12) were devoted to this specific transaction:

> Two sheep, for/by the hand of Etel-pī-Marduk,
> with respect to expedition of the five charioteers from Aleppo
> together with a troop of conscripts:
> to enable their expedition
> to inspect the camp of the Elamite soldiers.[3]

Despite the text's brevity, in these short lines lie marvels: a diviner peered into the mantic realm to make sure it was safe for five elite military officers from Aleppo – more than 900 km northwest of the fortress – to travel a short distance to visit encamped Elamites whose homeland was about 400 km to the east.

Questions abound: In a time when the kingdom of Babylon had been out of diplomatic touch with Aleppo and Elam – as well as literally every other state across the Near East – how and why had mercenaries from these far-flung places come to be in Babylonia? Why were men from Aleppo 'inspecting' an Elamite camp? And why was a ritual procedure of sheep-liver divination (Akkadian *bârûtu*) needed to make possible their expedition from the fortress (*dūrum*) to the camp (*karāšu*)? They were, after all, armed soldiers (eren$_2$ *piḫrim*) travelling from one fortified place within the kingdom to another.

Let us take a further example of divination used to authorize travel, from a longer and more detailed document, CUSAS 29 206, describing for the king an expedition of troops sent with more than 200 animals (oxen, sheep, goats, lambs and rams) to the nearby city of Nippur. This report identified that both the outbound and return journeys had to be authorized by a positive divination report. First, the expedition began with a military commander visiting the house of a female diviner (*bītim <ša> ša'iltim*), for an initial procedure.[4] The commander then reported to the fortress with sacrificial slaughterers, Suteans, and 'officials'.[5] The next day, a diviner marched with the commander at the head of the expedition where (upon arrival at Nippur) a second sacrifice and divination could be performed for the return trip, authorized only if the omens were 'favourable' (*ina uzu terētim šalmatim*; cf. CUSAS 29 62, where the results were 'invalid' (*nadî*)). Again we have to wonder why so much attention was focused on ascertaining favourable omens for a journey undertaken by armed soldiers from a royal fortress to a major city under Babylonian control which was as little as 12 km away. Much is clarified by context because these divinations (as we will shortly see) were just a few of many performed for the movement of people and goods across non-urban spaces in the kingdom. From other animal accounts, letters and even literary compositions, we can see that divination was routinely – and perhaps even primarily – used in this time and place as a kind of mantic administrative cross-check on the advisability of safe passage through the land.

For those wanting orientation, a brief explanation is in order. Sheep-liver divination (sometimes called 'extispicy' or 'haruspicy') was a common mantic practice of the ancient Near East, used from the 3rd millennium BCE into Late Antiquity, with variations appearing later in classical Greek, Etruscan and Roman culture, even surviving to the present day as a traditional craft in parts of Africa (see Koch 2018: 120–121 with nn 1–3). The apparatus for Mesopotamian extispicy runs into the thousands of documents (with several major sub-types of texts) and tens of thousands of individual omen readings – like some (but certainly not all!) mantic/religious forms, it is a heavily textualized type of knowledge – and so it is not possible or desirable to give a complete account of its history. But to give a basic sense of divination in its ideal form, a diviner (Sumerian: maš$_2$.šu.gid$_2$.gid$_2$, lit. 'one who reaches a hand (in)to the goat'; Akkadian: *bārû*, lit. 'inspector') first induced omens in (usually) sheep through ritual and prayer before conducting a sacrificial slaughtering; he then removed and inspected the liver and other organs of the animal, observing both expected conditions and abnormalities; and then, following an interpretation of the anomalies, came to a basic conclusion about the question for which the procedure had been performed: good, bad or inconclusive. Mesopotamian liver divination is reflected in a variety of texts, principally in the apparatus of the craft: clay models shaped like livers, giving instructions on how to read the ominous zones; compendia, which listed thousands of individual anomalies (holes, discolorations, *etc.*) and their meanings; and reports, which listed the results of individual liver readings. We also have a fair amount of information from state letters describing the roles of diviners and divination in statecraft and warfare; administrative texts documenting diviners' control of sheep and other economic resources; and even private contracts demonstrating their business affairs.

What attracts my attention here is the particular use made of divination in 17th century BCE Babylonia as a mantic window onto the non-urban landscape. In what follows, I will review the evidence for the use of divination in journeys and expeditions in the Late Old Babylonian setting. I will consider why this context of use is significant both for the histories of divination as a craft on the one hand, and for the history of Middle Bronze Age states on the other. Finally, I will explore how 17th-century divination went beyond taking topography and geography as topics of interest. Well beyond a tool for human agents to investigate terrain as a passive subject, divination created a living homology between craft and territory by formally integrating it into military-administrative practices and discursively assimilating it to natural and settled landscapes. It thereby became one of a number of acts of 'seeing' by the state – not only a form of surveillance but an ontology of sovereignty.

Mantic terrain, surveillant forts

We know already that diviners were stationed at many Babylonian fortresses of the 17th century BCE: attested not only at Dūr-Abiešuḫ, but also the fortresses of Kullizu,

Dūr-Iškun-Marduk, Dūr-Ammiditana and Bāṣum, and likely at some of the other 30 or 40 staffed and active fortresses of the kingdom.[6] The contexts in which diviners appear at Dūr-Abi-ešuḫ may give us a sense of their multiple roles in fortresses, since they are found not only in connection with divinations, but carrying out a range of administrative duties, sometimes attached to troop contingents (CUSAS 8 39; CUSAS 29 1, 8, 39, 40, 41, 145, and 152), or responsible for their provisioning (CUSAS 29 2–3), communicating directly with the king about military matters,[7] and sometimes acting as commanders, said to be authorized by royal commission (*ina pīḫat e₂.gal*).[8]

Diviners were therefore not mere apparatchiks for the soldiers and staff, but sometimes entirely responsible for these places. Their twin roles as ritualists and administrators were bound up in their control of the fortresses' animal herds, which sometimes numbered in the thousands.[9] They were regularly involved in everyday tactical operations but central to the very purpose of the forts: to see out into the unknown.

There are indications of very small temple cults in the Babylonian fortresses themselves, but no indication that diviners were connected to any of them.[10] Sacrifices to various divinities at Dūr-Abiešuḫ (mostly for journeys) which mention or were likely connected to divination do not mention temples or priests and were directed at deities other than the fortress' few temple deities.[11] Since divination did invoke or tacitly communicate with the gods and often used the same term for animal 'sacrifice' (*sizkur₂*), it would be a mistake to make an absolute distinction between divination and temple religion. But from an administrative and sociological point of view and for the purposes of this paper, the distinction is fully valid: diviners and divination were part of the military-administrative complex, not the 'religious' establishment.

Instead of 'sacrifices' of sheep to gods, what we find more commonly at the fortresses are sheep used for divination (CUSAS 29 42, 44–66). That the sheep were used for these purposes is made clear by the several features of the administrative texts, which record distributions of animals: the designation of the sacrificed sheep as udu u₂/*uṣurtum* ('sheep [with a divine] design [within]') or udu ꜱᴜᴅ(.ᴀ) (obscure, but perhaps referring to 'travelling' or to divination itself);[12] their designation as udu šu PN (lit., 'at the hand of PN', but perhaps by extension meaning '[for a] ritual act'); the phrase *ana nēpešti* (*bārîm*), 'for the ritual (of the diviner)'; and/or, more directly, the presence of diviners in the texts.[13]

The purposes of most of these divinatory procedures following on from the animal distributions was to check on the safe movement of troops out of the fortress and across the countryside to various destinations. The divinations all name specific troop units and identify the expeditions as the occasion: to Babylon, Nippur, Maškan-šāpir, other fortresses and the shrine of Parak-mār-Enlil (somewhere in the *very* immediate vicinity of Dūr-Abiešuḫ!).[14] But not only did they look to safeguard travel to specific cities and known place, but to and through unknown and ill-defined places as well: for 'journeys' (kaskal, *alākim*) to unspecified places, 'crossing into the countryside' (*ana libbi mātim*), travel by boat,[15] going 'upstream' (*redêm šūqqim*), and to the 'Elamite camp'.[16]

In all cases, the sheep sacrifices have to do with the movement of 'conscripts' (erin₂ *piḫrim*), animals, and/or grain from Dūr-Abi-ešuḫ to some other place. These divinations were rarely used for any purpose other than to authorize planned movement. The practice routinely anticipates that movement outside of the forts was the activity most in need of divine aid and intelligence and implies that the territory in between the forts and the cities – perhaps not in full control of the Crown – had the consistent potential to be hostile.

Other divinations at Dūr-Abiešuḫ for forts and cities *per se* (rather than for the territory in between them) impart a similar sense of danger for the lands outside the walls: one divination was performed 'for the safety of the city' (*ana šulum āli*) and another for 'the fort' (bad₃; CUSAS 29 64 and 162, respectively;[17] even one simple list of farming tools concludes with a reference to an 'omen of the flesh' (uzu *tēretim*), implying that even routine local farming activities on nearby land were conducted only on the 'permission' of auspicious results (CUSAS 29 124:9).[18] Other letters which do not mention divination nevertheless echo the sense of danger, with even armed men themselves needing escorts (lu₂ *ālik*) for travel, and in one case noting that among those watching over animals 'in the pasture there are those who are afraid of the enemy' (Béranger 2019, 103, 106). Actual divinatory reports from the very last days of the dynasty were even conducted to check on the advisability of bringing grain within the walls of the city of Babylon (Richardson 2002, 229–230).

All these topical concerns – about movement in open country, and the safety of the kingdom's forts, cities and hinterlands – are mirrored in a literary *tamītu*-oracle from Neo-Assyrian Nimrud known as BOQ 1. I have shown that this oracle is in fact a genuine artefact descending from Late Old Babylonian sources, speaking about exactly this same military insecurity in the countryside at the time of Samsuditana, specifying the same concerns and their solution via divination (Richardson 2019b). The oracle appears to have been crafted from original divinatory queries and letters about them (see Richardson 2005 for the 'Trouble' letters). Most astounding of all is how well the oracle preserves, a thousand years after the fact, the ambient fear about moving through unsafe terrain.

This divinatory attention to expeditions and movement is echoed by other texts which do not specifically mention the ritual, *e.g.*, in texts documenting various journeys out of Dūr-Abi-ešuḫ,[19] where a sense of constant movement pervades even the most pedestrian texts. For instance, the occasions on which grain rations were distributed to troops there almost always specify that the troops had just arrived from elsewhere, styled as grain given '*when* [troop unit X] stayed in [*i.e.*, was garrisoned in] GN', *inūma ... wašbu*. Given the regularity with which divinations were performed for other outbound travel, we may presume that incoming traffic to the fortress had been given prior approval for travel through similar procedures of sacrifice and divination at their points of expedition.[20] Further, the many messengers, envoys, runners, heralds, and couriers arriving to and departing from Dūr-Abiešuḫ were part of the same larger system of communication across space.[21]

These 'scouts' (*āmirū*) (CUSAS 29 8, 17, 28, 39, 40) and 'watchguards' (*maṣṣar(t)ū*) (CUSAS 29 141) of the forts were also fundamentally employed in the same project of landscape surveillance as the diviners, only using different techné, as was the use of various tribal contingents to report in on movements near their more remote settlements.[22] There was thus a nexus between divination, forts and surveillance over terrain. The systematic nature of this information complex is reflected in the occasions when forts notified Babylon of security threats. In the best-known episode of the year Ammiṣaduqa 15, a series of letters was sent to the king about marauding enemies in the countryside.[23] Of the three 'Trouble' letters for which the origin of information about these enemies can be traced, all three sources derive from fortresses (Bāṣum, Kullizu, and the Tigris fort).[24] In the case of the Tigris fort, the letter specifies that the role of the official in charge of the last-mentioned place was to 'keep watch' (*ḫâṭu*) and 'report' (*šapāru*) (AbB 1 2). The *raison d'être* of the fortresses was to maintain surveillance and communicate information to the centre; indeed, the very name of the Ḫaradum fortress denoted 'vigilance' (from Akk. *ḫarādu* B, 'to be alert, to keep watch').

The surveillance function may confound expectations that divination was fundamentally about futurity (*i.e.*, that it was a kind of 'fortune-telling'). Now, the purposes of these divinations were not about the (distant) future, given that what was being asked was whether an expedition leaving the fortress gates to go to a nearby place would arrive safely later that same day. But this short temporal focus actually comports with divination generally and in all ages: these omens were not about the far-flung future, but about revealing either already-existing conditions or events just around the corner, in the very near future (see Richardson 2010b, 247–248; on the limited period for which an extispical reading was considered valid (sometimes as little as a few days), see Heeßel 2010). Therefore what is particularly different about this use was its attention to landscape as its subject.

The combined associations of diviners, (in)security, fortresses, and reports evokes the image of a beleaguered state looking out over stateless lands, anxious to maintain security through the twin surveillances of enemy terrain through field reconnaisance and mantic knowledge. We may therefore speak of fortresses as having not only a project identity – military places filled with military people – but an epistemic discourse of 'seeing': systematic and explicit ways of knowledge managed through interlocking administrative, ritual, and textual practices.

Administrative praxis

Looking a little more closely at the practical contexts in which divination was used, it becomes clear that it was not merely a regular but a routinized part of administrative practice. That is, the individual texts we have probably only document discrete, single acts within a larger *chaîne opératoire*; it is not always possible to see how they fit into wider patterns of practice. For instance, at Dūr-Abiešuḫ, some texts link divination to the movement of personnel and goods while others simply document movement. In the case of the incoming troops units arriving to receive rations, we may assume that a divinatory procedure authorized their original outbound journey, but this is not recorded in the texts about incoming units.

Fortunately, it is possible to illustrate just how integrated divination was within military-administrative practice from the fortunate preservation of several texts relating to the fortress at Kullizum. Although they are not parts of the same transaction, they clearly represent individual steps within a single kind of administrative procedure. Together, they reveal the longer documentary chain by which fortresses were supplied with grain – and divination's role in that system. One is a letter (AbB 2 54) from the Babylonian king Ammiditana to officials at Sippar. The king writes to say that he has received a letter from 'the ones who are in charge' at Kullizum requesting 17,284 litres of grain for the troops for 'Month 9' (of an unspecified year); he orders the Sippar officials to in turn write to the Kullizum officials and prepare to receive porters who are to carry the grain – but only if a divination is performed and 'the omens are favourable' (*ina uzu terētim šalmatim*) – exactly the same terminology used in CUSAS 29 206, discussed above. The letter is then complemented by an administrative text (TLOB 1 19) documenting the release of 5163 litres of grain in Month 12 of the year Ammiditana 21 by some of the same officials mentioned in the letter, once again for the soldiers of the fortress of Kullizum. The release was effected by the 'instructions of a royal document' (*ana pī ṭuppi šarrim*), presumably a letter exactly like AbB 2 54. A third text is a divination report assignable to the archive of the Kullizum diviners (BM 97919). The text is fragmentary and the specific query it answered cannot be identified, but it is quite likely similar to the kind of report generated by the divinatory queries used at Dūr-Abiešuḫ to authorize travel. A fourth text (TLOB 1 18) shows us that the grain reserved for fortress provisioning was grown on lands owing rents to the palace and then held in readiness in the Sippar granaries and delivered in sometimes massive quantities; this consignment totalled more than 70,000 litres.

At a minimum, these texts, either attested or implied to have existed, document at least nine steps in the administrative chain of moving grain from the fields where it grew to the fortresses where soldiers ate it:

1. Grain from palace lands moved to granary reserves in Sippar (*e.g.,* TLOB 1 18)
2. Kullizum officials write a letter to the King
3. The King writes a letter to Sippar officials (*e.g.,* AbB 2 54)
4. Sippar officials write Kullizum officials
5. Diviners perform an extispicy, presumably precipitating:
6. an administrative text documenting the expenditure of sheep (*cf.* CUSAS 29 61)[25] and

7. a divinatory report reporting the results of the procedure (*e.g.*, BM 97919)
8. Sippar officials authorize release of grain from the *kārum* granary (*e.g.*, TLOB 1 19)
9. Bearers depart to carry grain from Sippar to Kullizum (*cf.* CUSAS 29 62)[26]

We do not have exemplary documents for every step of this procedure and cannot reconstruct it with complete precision. But especially given that diviners are attested in administrative roles at Kullizum,[27] it is likely that divinations were performed for some of Steps 1–4 and 8–9 of this procedural chain and not just the ritual of Steps 4–6 as stipulated by AbB 2 54. If we think that same set of procedures, including the divinations, were enacted once a month, every month, for at least some of the dozens of fortresses of the kingdom across the 17th century – and this just for grain shipments alone, to say nothing of troop movements, visits of officials, supply of equipment, reconnaisance missions, *etc*[28] – we have some sense of how deeply embedded divination was within administrative praxis.

And if we turn our attention to the range of applications to which divination was put at fortresses, we get an even stronger sense of how deeply it became enmeshed in daily administration concerning actions requiring passage over rural terrain: provisioning fieldworkers, supplying officials, resupplying other fortresses, sending booty back to Babylon, the performance of sacrifices and cultic journeys, inspections of camps, carrying letters to different cities, administering flocks, but with relatively few procedures accomplished for the purposes of 'well-being' or 'expelling evil' as generalized mantic protections (*e.g.*, CUSAS 29 59 and 64). Virtually every kind of occasion requiring movement outside of the walls of a fortress could require divinatory authorization and/or the oversight of a diviner – if indeed these were not one and the same thing.

The range of occasions for which divination was integrated into administrative procedures suggests that it was both familiar and necessary. Divination's sacrificial practices were linked (both anterior and posterior) directly to actions undertaken by a wide range of non-cultic personnel who depended on their resulting information. Grain could not be shipped, troops could not march and cultic sacrifices could not be brought to temples without the authorization of procedures whose interpretations rested in the hands of a very limited number of people. Divination's repetition as a quasi-public and routine administrative practice evokes the sense of Bourdieu's *habitus*, a socialized norm invested with economic, religious, and political capital. Its very regularity inscribed and reinscribed its authority with every use. Divination also spoke in a vernacular idiom comprehensible to the many different inhabitants and neighbours to fortresses who came from so many far-flung places across the Near East, from Qatna to Susa to Idamaraṣ to Uruk – and where fortresses had little in the way of temple establishments themselves. Most soldiers came from faraway places which had different tutelary gods and temple cults; the mercenaries staffing Babylonian fortresses in this time were identified by more than three dozen non-Babylonian ethnonyms, from Elamite to Gutian to *ḫāpiru* and beyond. But divination was a common-culture mantic form whose theological authority was not bound to a particular place or deity. In these and other respects, divination came to have a salience for the communities using it.

It may even be that the primacy of divination over temple cult came to be one of the ways in which fortress communities came to have a different sense of political community than the one modelled by Mesopotamian kingship. Traditional *šarrūtu* was ideologically formed on a fixed bedrock of city, temple, and palace; the warlord authority of fortress towns was based on a dynamic of mobility between fortified points. The first was authorized by deities enthroned in cellas; the second was authorized by the mantic surveillance of a living landscape crawling with allies and enemies. This brings us finally to my argument for the particular homology between divination and landscape that emerged as a form of 'sacred nature': a relational cosmos in which human animals and the land were communicants in a single analogistic system of meaning.

Wider historical context: politics and practices

It is clear enough by this point that divination had the particular function of landscape surveillance in 17th century BCE Babylonia. What wants more demonstration, however, is that this was a development new to the era rather than something 'baked in' to the practice itself. Let us make a quick review of divination's functions. When the Mesopotamian practice of sheep-liver divination first becomes textually visible to us, not later than ca. 2600 BCE, it is only because the term 'diviner' appears in a list of professions, where it is catalogued together with workers such as cooks and butchers – perhaps at this early point more of a craft than an art. By the last third of the 3rd millennium, however, royal literature shows us that divination was being used to choose priests and approve temple sites, more closely allied to formal cult practice. But then again by the Old Babylonian period (2004–1595 BCE), state letters show that divination had morphed once again and was now less clearly associated with temple cult, and more closely allied to statecraft and warfare. Extispicy over its first thousand attested years thus moved, as it were, from the kitchen to the sanctuary to the privy council;[29] it was not a practice with a fixed and singular use, though it remained essentially urban in its focus.

It should be emphasized, however, that a substantial shift even within the period in the mid-18th century changed how divination was used in military contexts. This shift in turn illuminates changes in not only the Babylonian state's structure but the scope of its ontology. Roughly speaking, divination's focus shifted from the vantage point of royal courts in major cities, using it to 'see' the doings of enemy kings and armies, to one of remote fortresses, using it to 'see' the doings of relatively local hinterlands. To explain this change, it is important to explain some of the political events which made the period after 1750 BCE so different from what came before and what this has to do with divination.

The post-1750 era was a difficult time for the First Dynasty of Babylon in more ways than one. Around 1737, the southern portion of the kingdom, including the wealthy city-states of Larsa, Uruk, Isin and Ur revolted against the Crown. The south was won back through a brutal reconquest, but the victory was an empty one: by 1720, most of the southern cities were abandoned, in whole or in part. The majority of the kingdom was lost. Babylon was left ruling just the core of small northern cities which had made up its entire kingdom only a century before. Babylon held control over this core for more than another century (down to 1595 BCE), but it did so in a geopolitical vacuum. Despite being almost continually in conflict with often-unnamed 'enemies', the Babylonian kings did not engage in diplomacy or warfare with any other royal state anywhere in the Near East from 1724 down to its demise in 1595 BCE. Perched on a small island of land in a sea of stateless territory, Babylon stood alone.

It is therefore the case that, although divination was consistently used for military purposes across the whole period, those purposes differed fairly radically before and after the watershed generation of 1750–1724. The divinatory texts and practices of 19th/18th-century Larsa, 18th-century Mari, and 17th-century Babylonia all give attention to protection from military dangers and the authorization of military victories. And the corpus of reports and letters from Mari already reflect that divination supplied mantic-military intelligence not only for conflicts between great state armies but also the safe passage of both soldiers and civilians across empty territory inhabited by lurking, unnamed enemies,[30] including in the important sense of gaining information not just about enemy people, but uncontrolled places and spaces. But after 1750 BCE, as Babylonian states collapsed one by one and as Babylon itself lost control over cities and territories, there simply were no more foreign kings, courts and states left to surveil. By the end of Samsuiluna's reign, only the deurbanized landscape and its hostile non-state inhabitants remained to be the subject of such inquiries about where and whether enemies 'out there' were moving.

Thus, although one could say with some justice that divination as a tool of military intelligence was in use in 1650 just as it had been in 1850, we see significant shifts in focus and application. I argue that this shift brought about two important changes. The first change was that the position of diviners in fortresses surveilling countrysides (rather than in palaces surveilling foreign courts and cities) reflected Babylonia's sharp reorientation away from a politics between peer states and towards a variety of non-state actors: tribes, mercenaries, *ḫabbātu*-bandits and stateless refugee populations. In this, divination was a barometer of the kingdom's geopolitical concerns, showing just how reduced its circumstances were. The second change was that the use of divination to peer into local but hostile landscapes so consistently generated an ontological homology between mantic knowledge and terrain; where reading a liver became an act of geomantic 'map-reading' more than a reading of the future, and where the landscape in turn became a stage where mantically-validated events played out.

The first claim is not so difficult to substantiate. There is little to no evidence for any diplomatic contact between Babylon and any other state after the middle of Samsuiluna's reign. We have substantial if scattered evidence that Babylonians occasionally came into contact with people from distant states throughout this 'long century' (primarily through trade), but none was sustained and none involved the palace. After 1724 BCE, the Babylonian kings never claim to have fought any conflict against anyone it (deemed to) call a 'king', mostly an assortment of (supposedly) leaderless and nameless 'enemies' and tribes. In the exceptional instances where names of enemy leaders were supplied, they were called 'generals' rather than 'kings' or given epithets like 'man of the lands'. In short, Babylon was not connected – as it had been so intensely in the time of Hammurabi – with other states through either diplomacy or war. We may posit that the state form begins to lose definitional coherence and integrity when it exists outside of any wider system of states.

Of course, some may prefer to understand that various 17th century enemies faced by Samsuiluna and his heirs were nascent dynasties which were simply unrecognized as such by Babylon: Kassites, the Sealand, Hana, *etc.* For two reasons I prefer not to follow this logic, however. For one thing, any such understanding must rely on no contemporary and only later evidence, the latter biased by retrospective claims of history and legitimacy. That is, it is all well and good in the 12th century BCE to look back and claim that someone named Gandaš was a 'king' of somewhere in the 18th century, but that by itself does not make it so. More urgently, however, the corollary of the observation that the 17th-century enemies and allies with which Babylon *did* treat were not royal as such is that they were not organized as state actors. The many mercenaries hired, 'enemies' fought, the many tribes allied in one moment and hostile the next were not: based in any city; with any temple or any palace; producing any royal literature or other symbols of legitimacy; exercising infrastructural powers of law, political membership, commerce, land ownership, *etc.* The point of this is not to argue that they were un- or under-developed; the point of this is that *legitimate kingship was not the exclusive form that political power of consequence took.*

That important political actors might be tribes or warlords with no pretensions to state rule is a supposition which not only makes sense of much of Babylon's history in this period, it even begins to explain the decline in royal literature, the restriction of state claims about territory and cult, and that the Babylonian king's power was increasingly based not on rule over cities, but rule over fortresses and countryside. To some extent, the problem was not only that Babylon was a 'failing state' but that the form of its rule increasingly mimicked the warlord groups which formed the basis of the Crown's power. In this respect, it would more surprising if divination's attention had *not* been steered towards such topics: fortresses, soldiers, insecure countrysides and 'enemies'. All this was simply a reflection of the culture's drift away from traditional kingship and closer to warlordism.

The second claim relates to divination as a form of knowledge about territory, an act of mental map-making. Babylon was no different from all pre-modern states in its limited ability but therefore dire need to make its land and people legible to it, in the way that James Scott has argued:

> The premodern state was, in many crucial respects, partially blind; it knew precious little about its subjects, their wealth, their landholdings and yields, their location, their very identity. It lacked anything like a detailed 'map' of its terrain and its people (Scott 1998, 2).

Especially in a changing geopolitical landscape in which state actors had demonstrated problems of access, divination both reflected and constructed what could be known about people and territory who were not clearly always either subjects or enemies.

On the one hand, divination paralleled military-administrative surveillance as acts of 'seeing' (through scouts, fortresses, watchtowers, *etc.*); but on the other hand, the liver itself mirrored the subject of its inquiry with its map-like features of an imagined built landscape. Diviners would examine a liver in a set order of zones and associated features. These included the following terms, given with their usual translation in divinatory texts first – some of which are openly geographic in their reference, some of which have alternative meanings in other contexts:[31]

> *bāb ekalli*, 'the Palace Gate'
> *danānu*, 'the Strength,' with the close by-form of *dunnu*, 'fort, fortified place'
> *dūr libbi*, 'the Fortress of the Heart'
> *kiṣirtu*, 'the Ridge', also in the same sense as a 'mountain'
> *manzāzu*: 'the Presence', but connoting also 'abode, whereabouts, resting place, military position'
> *maškanu*, 'the Emplacement,' also 'farming town, residence, tent'
> *mātu*, 'the Land'
> *nāru*, 'the River'
> *nīdi kussê*, 'the Throne Base'
> *nīru*, 'the Yoke', with in-text allusion to cities imposing a yoke on the land
> *padānu*: 'the Path', with the synonyms *ḫarrānum*, 'road, journey, travel, caravan, expedition(ary force), raid,' and *alaktum*, 'road, way'
> *pušqum*, a 'Constriction', also 'mountain defile, gorge, pass'
> *qarab-bītim*, 'the Storehouse'
> *rupšum*, 'the Width', also describing fields and canals
> *sūqi immerim*, 'the Passage of the Sheep', *i.e.*, a herding trail
> *ṣērum*, 'the Plain', *i.e.*, 'the steppe, open country'
> *šēpu*, 'the Foot', also 'approach, attack, transport, routing'
> *šubtu*, 'the Foundation', also 'settlement, village, dwelling place'.
> *ubānu*, 'the Finger', *cf. ubān šadî*, 'mountain peak'

These terms are only about half of all the major features and zones of the liver; one could not say that the system in its entirety was cartographic. Still, the terms flesh out the kingdom as a whole, radiating outward from the king's throne through the palace gate to the roads, villages, fortresses, rivers, hills, lonely farms and empty terrain.[32] And many of the other terms have been convincingly related to specific personnel (diviners, the army, shepherds, officials, the king), actions (military campaigns, invasion, rebellion) and themes (hostility, secrecy, hiddenness, chaos) occurring in the landscape of the liver. Many of the specific readings of anomalies in these same zones and features produced interpretive results such as raids, ambushes, abductions and enemies in the countryside and wild terrain. Altogether these are directly evocative of the *leitmotif* of a fortified but perilous landscape discussed in the earlier portion of this article. In successive Babylonian periods, the extrapolation of extispicy as a fundamentally cartographic mode of knowing – of the liver as a map – can be found in literary and scientific motifs of the zones of the liver reflected in the sky, or that the Sun god rising in the sky each day looked down on the land and read it like a liver.

   Fortress divination was therefore something like the 'Marauder's Map' from the *Harry Potter* series, a living tool which tracked events in space and time – an epistemic portal to knowledge about a socially-constructed landscape filled with dangers and possibilities. Divination materialized an analogized cosmos in which people, land, animals and divinity were bound up in a single system of reference. An important corollary of recognizing divination's primary aim of surveilling a landscape outside of the scope of state power and knowledge is that it was also less invested in futurity than one might assume. Divination was more closely concerned with revealing what already existed but was unknown, and less so with 'fortune-telling'.

Conclusions

I am no historian of religion, so I will not embarrass myself by trying to align these findings with particular formal or theoretical constructs; I will leave this to interlocutors more skilled in such analyses. I will make only a few concluding observations. The first is a very basic point, namely that analogies or other relations between the human social world and 'sacred nature' (or between humans and other-than-human beings) need not only emerge towards a holism, equation or 'positive' relationship in the construct of a relational cosmos. Late Old Babylonian divination communicated between people and a hostile and dangerous landscape, to mediate the dangers between those worlds. Analogism therefore should be understood to include negotiations of highly problematic or even openly hostile communities, whether social or natural.

   A second observation is to emphasize the differences between temple cult and divination. The two display more than just divergent formal apparatus, but different practices giving priority to completely different epistemic modes (*i.e.*, reciprocity versus knowledge) and ontological objects (*i.e.*, divine beneficence versus information about the world). Divination's focus became fundamentally spatial, a view onto surrounding but unknown landscapes, more than a temporal gaze towards the future.

   Third, I have argued that these differences in *mentalité* reflect a political environment changing under specific historical conditions. Within a few generations, Babylonian state society reorganized its access to other-than-human powers as the terms of sovereignty changed around it, from a landscape which was once populated by states, cities and armies into one which was rural, militarized and non-Babylonian. This change was not ideologically driven from the top-down but emerged from the bottom-up conditions of everyday state management: an endless loop of tracking enemies, keeping mercenaries loyal and trying to claw back control of a countryside which now imperilled the very cities which had once controlled it. Whether my specific interpretation or claim is correct in this respect may be less important, however, than a call to think about the development of 'relational cosmos' between human interlocutors and the other-than-human world partly as products of sometimes very local changes in the social, political and economic environment rather than as reifications of essential cultural principles embedded in deepest historical time. Pressures of change are not only possible, but unavoidable.

Notes

* Most abbreviations used in this essay follow the CAD (The Assyrian Dictionary of the Oriental Institute of the University of Chicago, 21 vols. [Chicago: Oriental Institute of the University of Chicago, 1956–2011]); other abbreviations include: CUSAS 8 = Van Lerberghe and Voet 2009; CUSAS 29 = Abraham and Van Lerberghe 2017; Haradum II = Joannès 2006; TLOB 1 = Richardson 2010a.

1 On the meaning of šu PN, see p. 58.

2 Abu-waqar na.gada in CUSAS 29 44, 46–48, 50–51, 56–58, 60, 63. Note also Abu-waqar s. Aḫu-waqar in the ration text CUSAS 29 2:21, 3:19, 8:2, and 39 (obv. 31'), in all cases listed immediately before or after diviners; this person is very likely identical to Abu-waqar na.gada.

3 *innepšu illikū* = 'to enable their expedition' (lit., '(that) their going could proceed'); *amārim* = 'to inspect' (lit. a 'seeing'). *Cf*, a divination performed for 'the man (carrying) the king's tablets with information about the Kassites reported by the Sutaeans' (CUSAS 29 65).

4 Note the 'account of rations for the household of the female diviner' (*qāti šuku é ša ša'ilatim*) within the archive of a Sutean man (TLOB 1 83a (Aṣ 12)).

5 The term for 'officials' (*šūt terētim*, lit. 'those of the message') connotes both an administrative sense (as: 'those charged with instructions') as well as a mantic one (as: 'those authorized by omens').

6 I have to date identified certainly 28 and possibly as many as 43 staffed and active fortresses in the Late Old Babylonian period (Richardson 2019a).

7 AbB 7 48, a letter nearly identical to the other 'Trouble' letters discussed in Richardson (2005) and (2019b); note also AbB 6 59–60.

8 AbB 2 54; TLOB 1 85–93a.

9 AbB 2 54 and 82; 3 22; 7 48 and 94; 14 179; TLOB 1 5, 85, 89, 91; with smaller numbers referenced in AbB 1 67 and 122, 2 82 and 86.

10 Ḫaradum had a small shrine to Adad and an offering place for Ištar (Ḫaradum II nos 2, 8, 49, 104), but no priestly titles are attested among its documents. A major purpose of Dūr-Abiešuḫ was to supply offerings for cults at nearby Nippur (see esp. CUSAS 8 23–38), but not for the shrines at the fortress itself, which included a (presumably) small temple to the gods Mišārum and (perhaps) Ninurta; a granary of the god Šulpae is also attested (CUSAS 8 7 and 60, 29 137). None of these texts mentions diviners or divination.

11 Notably, the Nippur gods for whom sheep were brought as šuku (CUSAS 8 23–38): Enlil, Ninlil, Ninurta and Nusku; these offerings were handled by priests titled nu.eš$_3$- and gudu$_4$-priests, not by diviners; conversely, those priests do not show up in the divination-related texts. See also CUSAS 29 44, 47, 67–68, 206; perhaps also 162–163. See also Béranger (2019), 106

12 The terms were not mutually exclusive; any given sheep might be called both u2 and/or sud(.A).
13 For these terms and translations, see the chapter on fortresses in my forthcoming book *For the Safety of the City.*
14 CUSAS 29 texts authorizing travel to Babylon, nos 44, 65(?), and 74(?); to Nippur, nos 45, 48, 50, 55; to Maškan-šāpir, no. 62; other fortresses, no. 44. On the texts and proposed reading for Parak(-mār)-Enlil, see Béranger (2019). *Cf.* CUSAS 29 146, documenting an expedition to Damrum with no mention of sheep or divination.
15 Including *itti* ma₂, ma₂.gur₈, ma₂.ḫi.a *še'im*, ma₂.i₃.dub.
16 CUSAS 29 texts authorizing travel for unspecified 'journeys', nos 47, 50; to the Elamite camp, no. 56; to the 'countryside', no. 48; by boat, nos 51, 54, 58 and 61 (destinations unspecified); 'upstream', no. 60.
17 *Cf.* CUSAS 29 59:6, *ana* [x] *nu-uk-ku-ri*; the translators offer 'for expelling evil(?)', but the writing is perhaps in error for *nukurti*, perhaps giving: *ana* [*māt*] *nukurti*, 'against the enemy land', another thema of BOQ 1 (see Richardson 2019b).
18 Compare against BOQ 1's concern that work could not be done safely perhaps even within 'one league, a half, or two thirds' from the city walls: see Richardson (2019, 230) and AbB 14 8:16, securing the harvest against the enemy from the *mēreš ālim*, the 'cultivation belt of the city'.
19 Expeditions of personnel other than the extispical texts are documented in CUSAS 8 21, 80; CUSAS 29 2, 3, 11, 17, 22, 25–28, 38, 74(?), 110, 146, 175(?), 176, 188, and 206, noting of no. 27 that travel provisions (ma₂.gar.ra) had to be given even for soldiers traveling from one part of the Dūr-Abi-ešuḫ complex to the other. Note also the ration texts given for the expeditions of units to other fortresses cited by Földi (2017), 17, nos 14, 15, and 27.
20 A few divinations sdo eem to have been performed upon the arrival of troops, *e.g.*, CUSAS 29 42; note also CUSAS 29 131:4, the eren₂ *ēribtum*.
21 See the titles lu₂ *ālik*, (ugula) lu₂.kaš₄.e, ra₂.gaba, *bēl/šūt teretim*, na.aš.bar, and nimgir; perhaps also (in this context) gir₃, as 'carrier'.
22 Information on Bimatî and Samḫarî troop movements was delivered by a 'translator coming from the Kassite camps' (ˡᵘ²*turgumannum ša ištu* e₂.ḫi.a eren₂ *Kaššî illikam*) and by Sutaean soldiers, respectively (AbB 7 47 and 10 150). A similar relay of information appears in CUSAS 29 65, where Sutaeans again deliver information (*ṭēmu*) about Kassite troops.
23 Similar reports from fortresses about local insecurity include letters (a.o.) from Dūr-Abiešuḫ (about an assault on Nippur; CUSAS 29 205), Bāṣum (outbound travel impossible despite the aid of a Sutean contingent: AbB 8 101), Dūr-Sîn-muballiṭ (report of an ambush and caravan travel cut off (AbB 8 24)), and perhaps Dūr-Iškun-Marduk.
24 *i.e.*, AbB 7 48, 10 150, and 1 2, respectively.
25 CUSAS 29 61 documents 12 sheep disbursed 'before the barley-carrying boats (can sail)'.
26 In this text, a divination is performed for the expedition of troops and bearers.
27 On the diviners at Kullizum, see further Richardson (2002, 229–230; 2010a, 58–69).
28 As at Dūr-Abiešuḫ texts, some administrative texts documenting procedures of movement and transport do not mention divination explicitly, but clearly required them a priori.
29 On this progression of textual focus, see Richardson 2010b: 226–235.
30 *E.g.*, ARM 26/1 20, 27, 29, 83, 96, 98, 100-bis, 101, 103, 112, 114, etc., alongside more general 'well-being' inquiries about the king, the cities, fortresses, and the 'district'. *Cf.* ARM 26/1 14, describing a difficult journey but not mentioning divination.
31 The extispical terms are discussed by Jeyes (1989, 51–96), while the allied meanings mostly follow CAD.
32 Jeyes (1978, 228) spoke of the reading of the zones of the liver as a 'learned geographical study', but without expanding on the idea.

References

Abraham, K. and Van Lerberghe, K. (2017) *A Late Old Babylonian Temple Archive from Dūr-Abiešuḫ: the sequel*. Bethesda MD, CUSAS 29.

Béranger, M. (2019) Dur-Abi-ešuh and the aftermath of the attack on Nippur: new evidence from three unpublished letters. *Revue d'Assyriologie* 113, 99–122.

Földi, Z. (2017) Cuneiform tablets and the antiquities market: the archives from Dūr-Abī-ešuḫ. *Distant Worlds Journal* 2, 7–27.

Heeßel, N. (2010) The calculation of the stipulated term in extispicy. In A. Annus (ed.) *Divination and Interpretation of Signs in the Ancient World*, 163–166. Chicago IL, Oriental Institute Seminars 6.

Jeyes, U. (1978) The 'Palace Gate' of the liver: a study of terminology and methods in Babylonian Extispicy. *Journal of Cuneiform Studies* 30 (4), 209–233.

Jeyes, U. (1989) *Old Babylonian extispicy: omen texts in the British Museum*. Leiden: PIHANS 64.

Joannès, F. (2006) *Les textes de la période paléo-babylonienne (Samsu-iluna-Ammi-ṣaduqa)*. Paris, Éditions Recherche sur les civilisations.

Koch, U. (2018) Converging fortunes – links between celestial and intestinal divination. In C.J. Crisostomo, E.A. Escobar and T. Tanaka (eds) *The Scaffolding of Our Thoughts: essays on Assyriology and the history of science in honor of Francesca Rochberg*, 120–147. Leiden: Ancient Magic and Divination 13.

Richardson, S. (2002) Ewe should be so lucky: extispicy reports and everyday life. In C. Wunsch (ed.) *Mining the Archives: festschrift for Christopher Walker on the occasion of his 60th birthday*, 229–244. Dresden: ISLET.

Richardson, S. (2005) Trouble in the countryside, *ana tarṣi* Samsuditana: Militarism, Kassites, And The Fall of Babylon I. In W. van Soldt (ed.) *Ethnicity in Mesopotamia* 273–289. Leiden: CRRAI 48.

Richardson, S. (2010a) *Texts from the Late Old Babylonian Period*. Boston, *Journal of Cuneiform Studies* Supplemental Series 2.

Richardson, S. (2010b) On seeing and believing: liver divination and the era of warring states. In A. Annus (ed.) *Divination and Interpretation of Signs in the Ancient World*, 225–266. Chicago IL, Oriental Institute Seminars 6.

Richardson, S. (2019a) Updating the list of Late OB Babylonian fortresses. New York, *NABU* 2019 (1.21).

Richardson, S. (2019b) The Oracle BOQ 1, the Dūr-Abiešuḫ texts, and the end of Babylon I. *Journal of Near Eastern Studies* 78 (2), 215–237.

Scott, J.C. (1998) *Seeing Like a State: how certain schemes to improve the human condition have failed*. New Haven CT: Yale University Press.

Van Lerberghe, K. and Voet, G. (2009) *A Late Old Babylonian Temple Archive from Dūr-Abiešuḫ*. Bethesda MD, CUSAS 8.

Chapter 5

Nymphs or trees? Some remarks on the 'animistic' interpretation of the *Homeric hymn to Aphrodite*, vv. 256-272

Doralice Fabiano

In this paper I investigate the more extensive and detailed description of nymphs in archaic Greek literature, a passage of the Homeric hymn to Aphrodite *(vv. 256-272) where nymphs' existence is depicted as tightly related to the life of trees. According to this text, nymphs are different from other gods because, although they are not subject to ageing, they are mortal. As nymphs are born and die, magnificent trees on mountains sprout and dry out. Special respect is paid to these trees that cannot be cut or damaged. Since Tylor's* Primitive Culture, *the most common interpretation of this archaic text understands nymphs as 'tree spirits', whose life depends on plants: when a tree is cut or dries out, for example, a nymph dies. This paper aims to challenge this traditional interpretation to suggest that trees are not nymphs' bodies, within the frame of a sharp opposition between spiritual and material, soul and body. Rather, as a thorough textual analysis shall show, in the* Homeric hymn to Aphrodite *trees can be considered as a sensible 'double' of the nymphs, that is a material object making nymphs visible to mortals. From this perspective, a parallel can be drawn between the function of trees in this specific passage and divine statues in a ritual context. This hypothesis can be indirectly confirmed by the absence of statues from nymphs' sanctuaries, while trees or gardens are more regularly attested, for example in cults founded or entertained by nympholepts, that is, men possessed by nymphs.*

Animistic beliefs in the *Homeric hymn to Aphrodite*: a brief historiographic overview

In the *Homeric hymn to Aphrodite*, nymphs are mentioned by Aphrodite in a very significant moment, when the goddess, who initially has presented herself as a young princess to Anchises, reveals her true divine identity, after their intercourse. Aphrodite assures her lover that he is now dear to the gods and predicts him the birth of their son, Aeneas. The nymphs of mount Ida will rear him during his early childhood and will bring him back to Anchises after five years. This last section of Aphrodite's speech (v. 256–272) offers maybe the most detailed description of nymphs in the extant ancient Greek literature.

> They associate neither with mortals nor with immortals,
> they live for a long time, and they eat immortal food.
> They put on a beautiful song and dance, even by the standards of the immortals.
> They mate with Seilênoi or with the sharp-sighted Argos-killer,
> making love in the recesses of lovely caves.
> When they are born, firs and oaks with lofty boughs
> spring out of the earth, that nurturer of men.
> Beautiful trees, flourishing on high mountains,
> they stand there pointing to the sky, and people call them the sacred precincts [*teméne*]
> of the immortal ones. Mortals may not cut them down with iron.
> But when the fate of death is at hand for them,
> these beautiful trees become dry, to start with,
> and then their bark wastes away, and then the branches drop off,
> and, at the same time, the soul [*psukhé*] goes out of the nymphs, as it leaves the light of the sun.

(*Homeric hymn to Aphrodite* 265–273, transl. Nagy 2018)

These verses attest that the existence of the goddesses is tightly related to the life of trees that sprout and dry out exactly when the nymphs come to life or die (*háma* 264, *homoû* 272). Since Tylor's *Primitive Culture* (1920, 2, 219–220; Hunt 2016, 29–71; 2018), this passage has been understood as the attestation (or, better, the survival) of an animistic stage in ancient Greek religion, when primitive mankind attributed a soul not only to human beings but also to plants, animals and objects. This phase in religious evolution was characterized by the direct worship of natural elements, considered as animated beings, and preceded the invention of fully anthropomorphic deities in the polytheistic stage. In Tylor's analysis, the consubstantiality of trees and nymphs proved not only that ancient Greeks worshipped sacred trees but also that trees were considered as nymphs' body and, conversely, nymphs were considered as the souls of trees (Hunt 2018, 238–239).

Through the mediation of Wilhelm Mannhardt's work, focused on the continuity between tree worship in antiquity and the folkloric traditions concerning trees in 19th century Europe (Mannhardt 1855–1857), Tylor's idea that nymphs were animistic personifications of natural elements and especially of trees has been passed down to one of the most influential scholars in Greek religion of the 20th century, Martin Persson Nilsson. In his *Greek Folk Religion* (1961), Nilsson argued that nature deities and, especially, the 'omnipresent' nymphs, were one of the most persistent features of 'popular' religion, testifying some kind of nature worship surviving in rural religion. Most recently, Jennifer Larson has continued to define nymphs as the embodiment of significant features of the local landscape (Larson 2007, 56).

Based on the description of nymphs in the *Homeric hymn to Aphrodite*, Larson also tries to provide a new understanding of these goddesses and of their relationship with trees within the framework of cognitive studies of religion (Larson 2019). She updates the classical notion of 'animism' by using Pascal Boyer's discussion of the 'minimally counterintuitive concepts' (Boyer 2001, 51–91) to clarify how a tree can be conceptualized at the same time as a tree and as a nymph. In Larson's view, nymphs are part of the reflective, 'mythological' beliefs generated by the (not always conscious) intuitive idea that springs, trees *etc.* are sentient beings. In her approach, however, intuitive thinking (*i.e.* trees are sentient beings) and mythological beliefs (*i.e.* anthropomorphic nymphs) are an inseparable unit and do not represent two consecutive stages of religious development, as they did for Edward Burnett Tylor (1920).

This paper aims to challenge this traditional interpretation of the description of the nymphs in the *Homeric hymn to Aphrodite*, to suggest that trees are not to be considered as nymphs' bodies, within the frame of a sharp opposition between spiritual and material, soul and body. Rather, as a thorough textual analysis shall show, in the hymn trees can be considered as a sensible 'double' of the nymphs, that is a material object making nymphs visible before mortals' eyes. From this perspective, I will argue that a parallel can be drawn between the function of the trees in this specific passage and statues of gods in cultic contexts. This hypothesis can be indirectly confirmed by the almost complete absence of statues from nymphs' sanctuaries, while trees or gardens are more regularly attested, for example in cults founded or entertained by nympholepts, *i.e.* men possessed by nymphs.

Mortal goddesses

The astonishing mortality attributed to nymphs in the *Homeric hymn to Aphrodite* is particularly important for the 'animistic interpretation' of these goddesses, because, for scholars who support this view, it proves that nymphs' existence depends on trees and suggests, therefore, their complete consubstantiality with the plants. Actually, (at least some) nymphs are immortal in archaic literature: Calypso, for example, is called goddess and immortal in the *Odyssey* (1, 51 and 5, 79–80, 97) and Maia is an immortal *theá* in the *Homeric hymn to Hermes* (154) (see Jaillard 2007, 28–39 on both). These different representations suggest that the particular focus on the mortality of nymphs in the *Homeric hymn* has to be understood as one depiction of nymphs among many possible others in Greek culture and that this passage has to be interpreted within the frame of this specific text.

I argue, therefore, that if nymphs' mortality is so heavily underlined in this context, it is precisely because the whole hymn is centred on the redefinition of the borders between mortals and immortals caused by the limitation of Aphrodite's powers (Rudhardt 1991). At the beginning of the hymn, in fact, Zeus gets angry with Aphrodite because the goddess forces the immortals to fall in love with mortal women and, by so doing, she continuously blurs the boundaries between mortals and immortals. Therefore, to limit his daughter's powers, Zeus makes her fall in love with Anchises and conceive a child, Aeneas. Only after undergoing the same humiliation she has caused to Zeus and other gods, does Aphrodite put an end to sexual intercourses between men and gods. This final decision deepens the gap between the two dimensions and restores solidarity between Olympians.

The narrative content of the hymn suggests that the accent on the mortality of nymphs is to be understood within the framework of the stabilization of boundaries between mortals and immortals. As several structuralist analyses have rightly underlined (Segal 1974; Strauss Clay 2006, 193–195), this element makes part of a complex pattern of oppositions arranged in a quadrangular scheme, where gods (who are immortal and forever young) occupy one pole and men (who are mortal and ageing) the other. Nymphs (mortal but exempt from ageing thanks to immortal food) are situated in a third pole, while Aphrodite evokes the unhappiest of all destinies (being immortal and subject to ageing) through the example of Tithonos, abducted by Eos, who obtained from Zeus immortality for her lover but forgot to ask for eternal youth. The presence of this hidden structure explains why the hymn underlines the mortality of nymphs and their function of mediation between men and gods: as paradoxical mortal goddesses, halfway between mortals and immortals, these divine beings fill the gap subsequent to the increasing and permanent separation of men and gods. The fact that at the end of the hymn Aphrodite orders Anchises to tell everyone that Aeneas' mother is a nymph (281–285), shows even more clearly, if need be, that nymphs are nearer to men than the Olympians, since their union with mortals seems to be more usual, not harmful for mortals and does not lessen the dignity (*timé*) of the goddesses (Rudhardt 1991, 16).

Moreover, the in-between nature of these divinities is functional to the specific task they receive from Aphrodite, that of being the nurturers of Aeneas; for the child, his stay with the nymphs is an intermediate step between the world of immortals, where he is born and where his mother belongs, and the earthly dimension of his father, where he is finally assigned. It seems like this is a necessary period of adaptation when moving down from one dimension to the other. From this perspective, the mountain inhabited by nymphs plays the same symbolic function as Zeus's thigh for the infant Dionysus, who, despite being the fruit of a mortal woman's womb, makes the inverse path from Thebes to Olympus, via his father's divine body (Romani 2004, 75–78; Pirenne-Delforge and Pironti 2022, 266–268).

Trees and nymphs

To better understand the nature of the relationship between trees and nymphs, it is noteworthy that the whole section of the *Homeric hymn to Aphrodite* concerning nymphs is centred on a striking series of similarities between the goddesses and the plants. The text first underlines the close resemblances between trees and nymphs (Olson 2012, 266), which are both 'beautiful' (261 *kalòn khóron*, 266 *kalaí*) and 'flourishing' (257 *bathúkolpoi*, 266 *teletháousai*). The exceptional height of the trees born with nymphs (264 *hupsikárenoi*) is also a divine attribute; in a previous passage, when Aphrodite reveals to her lover her divine identity, the goddess touches the roof of Anchises' hut with her head (173–174).

These implicit comparisons between trees and nymphs are founded on a widespread anthropomorphic representation of trees in Greek culture: the crown of trees is usually compared to the head and especially to hair (on the relationship between blooming, foliage and human hair see Empedocles DK 31 B 82; Pironti 2007, 198–199; Brulé 2015, 25–30, 71–72; Pilz 2019), their branches to arms, their roots to feet. It is worth noting that ancient philosophers use the same anthropomorphic model of a tree but they think of them as upside-down human beings, having their heads in the roots and their feet in the foliage (Repici 2000, 13–17). From that perspective, it is significant that the verb *keírousi* (268) is not commonly referred to the action of cutting down trees but, rather, to the cutting of hair. Moreover, in Greek culture, trees are mainly represented as feminine beings: tall, slender, with beautiful hair, they seem to exemplify an ideal image of female beauty (Frontisi Ducroux 2017, 95–10; *cf.* the simile of *Odyssey* 6, 161–163 between Nausicaa and a young palm in Delos).

Nymphs' mortality (or better longevity) and their arboreal nature are also strictly related. As Strauss Clay (2006, 195–196) has rightly observed, trees and especially their leaves that grow and fall according to the different seasons, are a common image to express at the same time the caducity of individual human life and its continuity through generations, as in the famous simile of *Iliad* 6, 146–149 (*cf.* 21, 462–466). Arboreal anthropogonies are also known in Greek culture (Hesiod, *Works and Days* 145) and some philosophers considered trees as the first living beings generated by Gaia (Empedocles DK 31 A 70, see Ferella 2019). In the hymn, nymphs, trees and humans share the same abode, the earth that nurtures all, that is the epichthonian dimension *[earthly]* (265). So, the tight association of nymphs with trees seems to be quite appropriate to the mortal nature of these divinities. However, the trees mentioned in the hymn are of a special kind, not only because of their exceptional size but also because both firs (*elátai*) and oaks (*drúes*) do not let their leaves drop during the year. This feature perfectly expresses the nature of nymphs as it is described in the hymn: as the trees are mortal but, because of their evergreen foliage, are not touched by the cycle of the seasons (Aristotle, *Longevity* 6, 467 a12), so the goddesses are doomed to die but they do not undergo the ageing process because of the immortal food they eat (260).

More generally, trees share with nymphs their exceptional longevity (Aristotle, *Longevity* 4). A fragment of Hesiod (fr. 304 Snell-Maehler = Plutarch, *On the failure of oracles* 415 CD), for example, possibly compares the extraordinary duration of nymphs' life to that of ten palms (*phoînix* but this term could refer also to the phoenix-bird), the most long-lived among trees, while Pindar used the expression *isodéndrou tékmar aiónos* ('a term of life equal to that of trees', fr. 165 Maehler = Plutarch, *On the failure of oracles* 11, 415 E) to qualify nymphs' longevity. Plutarch, who cites both fragments, relies on these texts not only to affirm the daemonic nature of nymphs in a platonic meaning, that is, their intermediary nature between men and gods, but also to underline their extraordinary longevity, a trait which is not explicit in the *Homeric hymn to Aphrodite*.

To sum up, features commonly attributed to trees in Greek culture (femininity, youth, longevity) mirror precisely the most distinctive qualities of nymphs within the pantheon and also in the spatial and temporal dimensions. Regarding space, trees, as the sacred precinct of the gods, mark the boundaries between mortals and immortals, just as nymphs occupy an intermediate position between men and gods; regarding time, trees, as nymphs, are more long-lived than men, forever young, yet doomed to die.

Living images

As mentioned earlier, classic animistic interpretations have found in the *Homeric hymn to Aphrodite* the proof that Greek nymphs were considered as trees' souls and *vice versa* that trees were considered as nymphs' bodies. Though this is not always made explicit, such a reading depends on the idea that the relationship between trees and nymphs is based on complete reciprocity; not only trees sprout and dry out when nymphs are born or die, but the reverse is also held for true in this view and nymphs are thought to be hurt or killed when trees are harmed or cut down. According to Tylor's reading of this passage, in the hymn 'the hamadryad's life is bound to her tree, she is hurt when it is wounded, she cries when the axe threatens, she dies with the fallen trunk' (Tylor 1920, vol. 2, 219 *cf.* Brulé 2012, 150–151).

The hymn indeed depicts the birth and the death of nymphs and trees as synchronic events (264 *áma*, 272 *omoû*). This suggests that the appearance of trees reflects what happens to nymphs or at least their cycle of life. However, the text never states the reverse idea that what happens to the plants directly affects the goddesses. If it is explicitly prohibited to cut down nymphs' trees (273), it is certainly because they form the precincts of the immortals: they cannot be removed because they are boundaries of a sacred space and not because this would cause nymphs' death. Later Hellenistic sources, such as Apollonius Rhodius and Callimachus confirm this reading: though inspired by our passage, they attest that the nymphs continue their life after their tree has been cut down. In the *Argonautica* (2, 475–483), for example, the nymph whose tree has been cut down, persecutes the descendants of her offender, while in the *Hymn to Delos* (79–85), nymphs are said to be happy when trees are green and unhappy when the plants let their leaves drop.

Based on these remarks and parallels, I argue that trees, far from being nymphs' bodies, are better to be understood as a kind of 'interface' or 'device' that makes visible the presence of the goddesses before mortals' eyes, also thanks to their resemblances with nymphs. This is also proven, in my view, by the fact that the whole description of the nymphs in the *Homeric hymn to Aphrodite* is built around the antithesis between visible trees and invisible goddesses. The first part of the passage

(259–263), in fact, depicts the divine life of nymphs, who dance with gods and mate with silenoi but out of men's sight. The second part (266–271), on the contrary, deals with the aspects of nymphs that are more perceptible to mortals, such as their life cycle or their function as *teméne* of immortals, which show their intermediate nature between gods and humans.

Based on these considerations, I suggest that the role of trees can be paralleled with that of cult statues which make gods present within a certain place, without, however, being the gods (Pirenne Delforge 2008; 2014; Collard 2016). From that perspective, it is very significant that cult statues are usually absent from nymphs' cult places and especially from nymphs' sacred caves (Sporn 2010), while luxurious vegetation (also if not always trees) is one of the most recurrent features (Calame 1999, 153–174, Brulé 2012, 17–19, 204–206).

To support this reading, I would like to mention two archaeological sites where nymphs' cult is attested and where the inscriptions found *in situ* suggest that vegetation had to play an important role in 'representing' the goddesses. The first is the sacred cave of Vari (Attica), on Mount Hymettos (Weller 1903; Connor 1988; Purvis 2003, 31–60; Schörner and Goette 2004; Pache 2011, 45–52; Fabiano 2013; Gillis 2021, 195–200). The cave, whose cultic activity is attested from the archaic period to the 2nd century CE, was dedicated to the nymphs, along with Pan, Apollo, possibly Hermes and the Charites. According to one of the inscriptions carved on a block of rock (IG I³ 980) and dated approximately to the third quarter of the 5th century BCE, a man named Archedamos and coming from Thera worked out the interior of the cave following the instructions he received directly from the nymphs. In the same inscription, Archedamos, who probably was a quarryman (Gillis 2021, 197), defines himself as a man possessed by the nymphs (*nymphóleptos*). This kind of theolepsy is well attested in Greek religion, mainly known by the Platonic description in the *Phaedrus* (238 c–d), where Socrates is seized by the goddesses after unwittingly entering their sanctuary on the banks of the Ilissos and ascribes to them his unusual eloquence. Archedamos certainly organized the sacred space of the cave by carving steps, niches and possibly by sculpting a seated figure, now headless, very damaged and therefore impossible to identify (ancient travellers in the 18th century interpreted it as Cybele sitting on a throne with two lions). The name of Archedamos is inscribed multiple times on the walls of the cave, in different spellings, apparently to 'sign' his work. This is even more striking in a relief sculpted on a wall at the bottom of the cave, where Archedamos represented himself with his work tools before an altar where the names of Apollo and possibly of Hermes are inscribed (Connor 1988; Gillis 2021, 195). As he states in another inscription (IG I³ 977 B), with his work Archedamos intended to build a house for a (single and unnamed) nymph (*exoikodómesen*, a term which would be better translated as to 'complete' or 'perfect' an already existing house). The emphasis he put on his own representation through the relief and on his work through the inscriptions suggests that Archedamos presented himself as the founder of this cult, directly invested in this role by the nymphs who possessed him.

The architectural modifications of the natural space of the cave, therefore, were intended as a strategy to make visible the presence of the nymphs before worshippers' eyes. Vegetation was an essential part of this plan; according to another inscription (IG I³ 977 A), Archedamos, planted a *kêpos* 'garden' for the (plural) nymphs. In Greek culture, gardens are eroticized spaces, especially linked to Eros, Aphrodite and the sphere of seduction and marriage, to which the nymphs also belong (Motte 1973; Calame 1999, 157–164; Borgeaud 2013). More interesting for our purpose, in ancient culture gardens were orchards, especially characterized by the presence of fruit trees (*e.g.* the garden of Alcinous at *Odyssey* 7, 114–116). We can therefore suggest that Archedamos possibly considered these plants as a means to make the nymphs present in the sacred space, because of the tight link between the goddesses and the trees.

The second example of trees and plants as a sort of device for representing nymphs comes from another sacred cave, that of Pharsalus in Thessaly (Decourt 1995, 88–94; Wagman 2011; 2016; Borgeaud 2013). An inscription (Wagman 2016, n. 1, 57–65), dated to the first half of the 5th century BCE and carved halfway up the ascent of the cave, contains the dedication made by a certain Pantalkes of a 'work' (l. 3 *érgon*) – presumably the stairway that gave access to the sanctuary – and the mention of a laurel (l. 4 *dáphnan*), though the context of this second element is very unclear.

A second inscription (Wagman 2016, n. 11, 66–93), carved about a century or more after the first dedication, contains a long hexametric poem addressing the visitors of the cave. The text first numbers the divinities worshipped in the cave: nymphs are mentioned in the first place, along with Pan, Hermes, Apollo, Heracles, and then comes to a second group of gods linked to health and healing, such as Chiron, Asclepius, and Hygieia. After, the epigram lists the votive that the visitors are expected to see in the cave: significantly, plants (l. 9 *émphuta*) are mentioned in the first place, before depicted tablets, statues, and other gifts. In a second section, the poem describes how these deities inspired Pantalkes to found (or maintain) the shrine and lists the rewards he received from each one in return for his work. The verses concerning the nymphs (ll. 10–13) are especially interesting to my purpose:

> The nymphs who tread these lands endowed Pantalkes with a noble heart and made him their overseer: he is the one who planted (l. 12 *ephúteuse*) this place and toiled over it with his hands; and they rewarded him in return with bountiful living through all of his days. (transl. Wagman 2016, 68)

In this section, two elements are especially noteworthy: in the first place, it is remarkable that the action of planting is rewarded precisely by the nymphs among all other mentioned divinities, which suggests that these plants were especially intended to please them and reinforces, if need be, the tight link between these goddesses and the vegetation. The second element I shall highlight is that the role of guardian of the shrine of nymphs (*epískopos*) is represented as a form of 'gardening' or, at least, there is an equivalence between founding a shrine for the nymphs and entertaining it, on the one hand, and taking care of vegetation on the other hand.

Conclusions

The *Homeric hymn to Aphrodite* provides a valuable source for redefining the association between nymphs and trees. A careful analysis shows how difficult it is to accept a classic animistic interpretation of this text; as we saw, nymphs' biological cycle, so to speak, is reflected by the variation in trees' aspect, while modifications of trees do not necessarily affect nymphs' existence. This invites us to find elsewhere models for the relationship between the goddesses and the plants. As the archaeological testimonies of nymphs' cults mentioned above have suggested, from an emic perspective a pertinent element of comparison for nymphs' trees could be the cultic statue, as a device to make the goddesses present before worshippers' eyes.

I shall also add that, if the bond between nymphs and trees is so tight, it is also because trees can show another characteristic of nymphs' power, their being literally 'rooted' in the local space. According to a famous Platonic definition (*Phaedrus* 262 c–d), nymphs belong to the category of the *entópioi theoi* 'the gods of this specific place/landscape'. It is therefore possible to suggest that nymphs, as local divinities, are considered as deeply grounded in a specific territory in the same way as are the natural elements. In ancient scientific thought, in fact, trees, uninterruptedly fed by the earth through their roots, can be represented as embryos who never leave their mother's womb (Repici 2000, 18; Ferella 2019, 82). From this perspective, it is significant to remark that nymphs, like plants, never move from their abode. In the *Iliad* (20, 7–10), for example, when Zeus tells Themis to summon all the gods to a council, the poet, to show that nobody can refuse to obey Zeus's orders, underlines the extraordinary presence of nymphs and rivers. It is also because of this strong relation to particular and significant places that nymphs appear to be primarily involved in the integration of foreigners (maybe such as Archedamos in Attica or Adamas in Paros, see Larson 2001, 179–180; Purvis 2003, 33–34) into a territory or in the re-integration of individuals who have been far away from home for too long into a society (Malkin 2001; Fabiano 2021).

To sum up, trees in Greek religion cannot be considered as nymphs' bodies. However, it should further be noted that these natural elements can neither be considered as passive and inert objects in the perspective of what Descola has called naturalism, a kind of ontology distinctive of Western thought and, in his view, directly derived from ancient Greece (Descola 2013, 63–67, 172–174, 199–200). Actually, the existence of this category has been criticized and many anthropological works on contemporary European society show that activities such pet-keeping or, of more significance to my purpose here, gardening continuously transgress the boundaries between humans and non-humans (Degnen 2009; Candea and Alcayna-Stevens 2012). So, in analysing the dossier of nymphs' trees in Greek religion, it would be more useful to abandon both the categories of animism (broadly intended as the tendency to 'humanize' non-human world) and naturalism (the tendency to deepen the gap between human and non-human world), to focus on the 'gardening activity' implied by the association of trees and nymphs in nymphs' cult as a means through which humans build the relationship with gods. From that perspective, at a general level, taking care of plants (not cutting them, planting them or consecrating them) seems to be in the first place the homologue of the 'care' humans owe to divinities. This is indirectly confirmed by the use of terms such as *therapeîa* in Greek ('service paid to gods') and *cultus* in Latin: both terms can refer to gods and plants (for the occasional use of *therapeîa* in the sense of 'taking care of plants' see Plato, *Theetetus* 149e and Theophrastus, *Enquiries into plants* 2, 2, 12). Of course, that 'care' is not specifically owed to nymphs, but to divinities in general.

However, the 'care' implied by gardening in nymphs' cult also hints at specific characteristics of nymphs in Greek religion, especially at the relationship they are expected to have with humans. In the first place, the action of planting seems to reflect the fact that nymphs as local deities are thought to 'root' individuals in a specific territory, as I suggested before. Secondly, nymphs, as courotrophic deities, are especially connected with the development of children which, in many societies is represented as a process equivalent to growing plants (Ingold 2000, 77–88; for ancient cultures see Bretin-Chabrol 2012, 233–398; Buccheri 2012). From this point of view, gardening could be considered as an activity particularly appropriate for the goddesses because of its similarity to the kind of actions humans attributed to them. These considerations suggest that the more significant part of the relationship between trees and nymphs in Greek religion is not in some degree of identification of these two elements, but rather in the similarity of the actions that humans make to come into contact with both of these non-human worlds.

References

Borgeaud, P. (2013) Sagesses de jardiniers. In D. Barbu, P. Borgeaud, M. Lozat and Y. Yolokhine (eds) *Mondes clos. Cultures et jardins*, 105–118. Lausanne, Gollion.

Boyer, P. (2001) *Religion Explained. The Evolutionary Origins of Religious Thought*. New York, Basic Books.

Bretin-Chabrol, M. (2012) *L'arbre et la lignée: métaphores végétales de la filiation et de l'alliance en latin classique*. Grenoble, Millon.

Brulé, P. (2012) *Comment percevoir le sanctuaire grec ? une analyse sensorielle du paysage sacré*. Paris, Les Belles Lettres.

Brulé, P. (2015) *Le sens du poil (grec)*. Paris, Les Belles Lettres.

Buccheri, A. (2012) Costruire l'umano in termini vegetali: *phyo* e *physis* nella tragedia greca. *I Quaderni del ramo d'oro* 5, 137–165.

Calame, C. (1999) *The Poetics of Eros in Ancient Greece*. Princeton NJ, Princeton University Press.

Candea, M. and Alcayna-Stevens, L. (2012) Internal others: ethnographies of naturalism. *Cambridge Anthropology* 30 (2), 36–47.

Collard, H. (2016) *Montrer l'invisible : rituel et présentification du divin dans l'imagerie attique*. Liège, Presses Universitaires de Liège.

Connor, W.R. (1988) Seized by the Nymphs: nympholepsy and symbolic expression in Classical Greece. *Classical Antiquity* 7(2), 155–189.

Decourt, J.-C. (1995) *Inscriptions de Thessalie I: les cités de la vallée de l'Énipeus*. Athènes, École française d'Athènes.

Descola, P. (2013) *Beyond Nature and Culture*. Chicago IL, University of Chicago Press.

Degnen, C. (2009) On vegetable love: gardening, plants, and people in the north of England. *Journal of the Royal Anthropological Institute* 15 (1), 151–167.

Fabiano, D. (2013) La nympholepsie entre religion et paysage. In P. Borgeaud and D. Fabiano (eds) *Perception et construction du divin dans l'Antiquité*, 165–195. Genève, Droz.

Fabiano, D. (2021) Les Nymphes et l'enjeu du territoire. Une lecture d'Euripide. *Électre* 774–858. *Revue de l'histoire des religions* 238(3), 461–499.

Ferella, C. (2019) Empedocles and the birth of trees: Reconstructing P.STRASB. GR. INV. 1665-6, ENS. D-F 10B-18. *Classical Quarterly* 69(1), 75–86.

Frontisi-Ducroux, F. (2017) *Arbres filles et garçons fleurs: métamorphoses érotiques dans les mythes grecs*. Paris, Seuil.

Gillis, C. (2021), *Des dieux dans le four: enquête archéologique sur les pratiques religieuses du monde artisanal en Grèce ancienne*. Villeneuve-d'Ascq, Presses Universitaires du Septentrion.

Hunt, A. (2016) *Reviving Roman Religion: sacred trees in the Roman world*. Cambridge, Cambridge University Press.

Hunt, A. (2018) Arboreal animists: the (ab)use of Roman sacred trees in early anthropology. In E. Varto (ed.) *Brill's Companion to Classics and Early Anthropology*, 231–254. Leiden/Boston, Brill.

Ingold, T. (2000) *The Perception of the Environment: essays on livelihood, dwelling and skill*. London/New York, Routledge.

Jaillard, D. (2007) *Configurations d'Hermès: une théogonie hermaïque*. Liège, Centre International d'Étude de la religion grecque antique.

Larson, J.L. (2001) *Greek Nymphs: myth, cult, lore*. New York, Oxford University Press.

Larson, J.L. (2007) A land full of gods: nature deities in Greek Religion. In D. Ogden (ed.) *A Companion to Greek Religion*, 57–70. Malden MA, Blackwell.

Larson, J.L. (2019) Nature gods, nymphs and the cognitive sciences of religion. In T. Scheer (ed.) *Natur–Mythos–Religion in Ancient Greece*, 71–85. Stuttgart, Steiner.

Malkin, I. (2001) The Odyssey and the nymphs. *Gaia* 5, 11–27.

Mannhardt, W. (1855–1857) *Wald- und Feldkulte*. Berlin, Gebrüder Borntraeger.

Motte, A. (1973) *Prairies et jardins de la Grece antique: de la religion à la philosophie*. Bruxelles, Academie royale de Belgique.

Nagy, G. (2018) The homeric hymn to Aphrodite, https://archive.chs.harvard.edu/CHS/article/display/5293.

Nilsson, M.P. (1961) *Greek Folk Religion*. New York, Harper.

Olson, D.S. (2012) *The Homeric Hymn to Aphrodite and Related Texts: text, translation and commentary*. Berlin/Boston, de Gruyter.

Pache, C.O. (2011) *A Moment's Ornament: the poetics of nympholepsy in ancient Greece*. New York, Oxford University Press.

Pilz, O. (2019) Water, moisture, kourotrophic deities, and ritual hair cutting among the Greeks. *Les études classiques* 87, 111–124.

Pirenne-Delforge, V. (2008), Des marmites pour un méchant petit Hermès! Ou comment consacrer une statue. In S. Estienne, D. Jaillard, N. Lubtchansky and C. Pouzadoux (eds) *Image et religion*, 103–110. Naples, Publications du Centre Jean Bérard.

Pirenne-Delforge, V. (2014), Des dieux parmi les hommes: l'installation des « statues de culte » en Grèce ancienne. *Techne* 40, 30–34.

Pirenne-Delforge, V. and Pironti, G. (2022) *The Hera of Zeus: intimate enemy, ultimate spouse*. Cambridge/New York, Cambridge University Press.

Pironti, G. (2007) *Entre ciel et guerre: figures d'Aphrodite en Grèce ancienne*. Liège, Presses Universitaires de Liège.

Purvis, A. (2003) *Singular dedications. Founders and innovators of private cults in classical Greece*. New York, Routledge.

Repici, L. (2000) *Uomini capovolti. Le piante nel pensiero dei Greci*. Bari, Laterza.

Romani, S. (2004) *Nascite speciali: usi e abusi del modello biologico del parto e della gravidanza nel mondo antico*. Alessandria, Edizioni dell'Orso.

Rudhardt, J. (1991) L'hymne homérique à Aphrodite. Essai d'interprétation. *Museum Helveticum* 48 (1), 8–20.

Schörner G. and Goette H.R. (2004) *Die Pan-Grotte von Vari*. Mainz am Rhein, Von Zabern.

Segal, C. (1974) The Homeric hymn to Aphrodite: a structuralist approach. *The Classical World* 67 (4), 205–212.

Sporn, K. (2010) Espace naturel et paysages religieux: les grottes dans le monde grec. *Revue de l'Histoire des Religions* 227 (4), 553–571.

Strauss Clay, J. (1992) *The Politics of Olympus: form and meaning in the major Homeric hymns*. London, Bristol Classical Press.

Tylor, E.B. (1920) *Primitive Culture. Researches into the Development of Mythology, Philosophy, Religion, Language, Art, and Custom*. London, Murray.

Wagman, R.S. (2011) Building for the nymphs. *Classical Quarterly* 61 (2), 748–751.

Wagman, R.S. (2016) *The Cave of the Nymphs at Pharsalus: studies in a Thessalian country shrine*, Leiden, Brill.

Weller, C.H. (1903) The Vari Cave. *American Journal of Archeology* 7 (3), 263–300.

Chapter 6

The dawn of the *Potnia.* Reception and re-interpretation of an archetypal model in protohistoric peninsular Italy

Valentino Nizzo

This contribution aims to deepen the complex iconographic dossier of Potnia theron[1] by focusing attention on its early stages of reception in protohistoric peninsular Italy. The analysis of the mode of recognition and elaboration of this mythical archetypal model offers important insights for the understanding of cultural and religious dynamics of interaction among the proto-historic populations of ours Peninsula, central Europe and the Mediterranean world during the 8th century BCE.

Contemporary *Potnia*

Cultural anthropology has long highlighted how objects, even the most common, as well as images can have their own social life and their own 'agency'.[2] Their ability to interact with reality varies over time and is conditioned by the 'context' in which the interaction takes place and by the identity of the 'receiver', according to the terminology developed by Roman Jakobson in his influential reconstruction of the communication functions (Jakobson 1960). The 'message' that they convey and/or pre-suppose can also vary over time and even profoundly change with respect to what were its original communicative purposes. To interpret the nature, meaning and/or function of objects and images, it is therefore always appropriate to try to investigate their evolution over time, trying to trace their possible archetypes.

For these reasons it may be useful to begin this paper with a provocation: the contemporary image of an archaeologist, Nunzia Laura Saldalamacchia (Fig. 6.1). She holds a PhD and is specialized in the study of amber fibulae and protohistoric jewels. Nunzia also became a jewellery designer inspired by the jewels she had studied.[3] With great pleasure I wanted some of her creations to be available in the Villa Giulia bookshop in Rome. In the photo she is wearing an iconographic motif characteristic

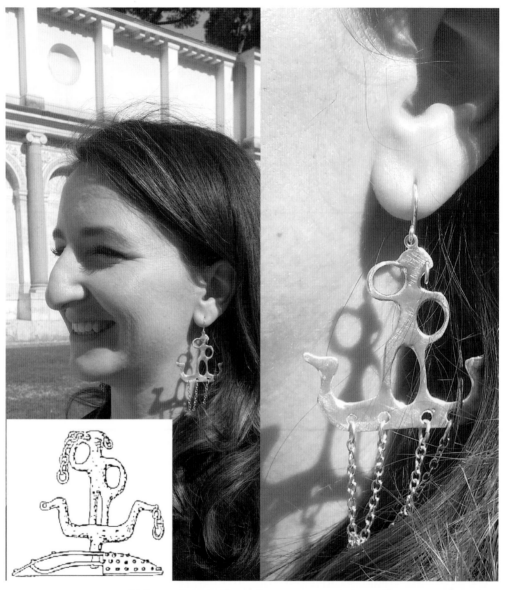

Fig. 6.1: Nunzia Laura Saldalamacchia at Villa Giulia wearing an earring of her invention inspired to the early Iron Age Campanian metallotechnic. (photograph: Author); bottom left: a Villanovan censer lid with anthropomorphic figure from Suessula, National Archaeological Museum of Naples, inv. 3252 (From Horsnaes 2001, 18, fig. 7).

of the early Iron Age Campanian metallotechnic. In the motif we can recognize a hybrid anthropomorphic figure which had already attracted my attention when I was in charge of the publication of some bronze pendants from the Gorga's collection kept at the Museum of Etrusco-Italic Antiquities of the Sapienza University of Rome (Nizzo 2007).

My colleague Nunzia wished to transform these objects into a pair of earrings. The object was originally used as a pendant or applied as a decorative element on rare parade fibulae or on particularly valuable metal vases, such as the traditional Villanovan censer (incense burner).[4] In my opinion, this image allows us to reflect immediately on a very important conceptual aspect which is the purposes of this paper as mentioned above: images have their own history and evolution. There may be discrepancies between the original idea of who made and constructed images and the interpretation of the images themselves; this difference may depend on the support or context with which they are associated, especially in the case of jewellery and ornaments made to be worn and exhibited. The meaning of some images can therefore be enriched and changed over time, also depending on the viewer's perspective or the circumstances of the observation. The images can therefore have eternal life and can be manipulated, also distorting their original meaning (Hodder 1982, 10).

Context has a profound influence on how an image is processed and received. The perception of its meaning can change according to the 'social life' of the objects to which the image is associated and their various possible destinations. This includes their final arrival in the contemporary world, as shown by the jewel worn by Nunzia Laura Saldalamacchia who is perfectly aware of its original meaning and has also chosen it to emphasize their common origins in Campania. This last consideration highlights one more issue that I would like to address in my report: it should never be taken for granted that the users of objects like these fully understand their meaning, as well as those who made the object.

Some of the case studies that I will report during this paper demonstrate how the indigenous artisans have often drawn inspiration from prototypes made elsewhere and have adapted them more-or-less freely to the needs and sensibilities of the local customer. We have some evidence to hypothesize that these craftsmen have not always been able to grasp the original meaning of their models.

Looking for the *Potnia*

This paper develops and updates a study initiated in 2007 starting from an absolutely inorganic nucleus of objects collected by the famous tenor Evan Gorga (1865–1957) at the end of the 19th and beginning of the 20th century.[5] Unfortunately, there was no information about the place and context of discovery. Their cultural, artistic and chronological framework could therefore only be carried out on a stylistic basis (Fig. 6.2). However, thanks to comparisons with similar finds, it was possible to say that the area of origin of this objects covered almost all of the Italian Peninsula and their chronology ranged from the 8th to the 6th century BCE.

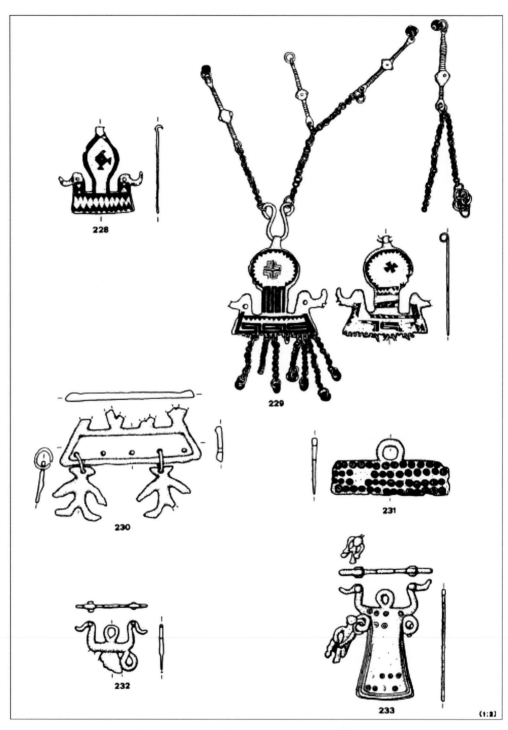

Fig. 6.2: Bronze pendants from the Gorga Collection kept at the Museum of Etrusco-Italic Antiquities of the Sapienza University of Rome (from Nizzo 2007, 343, tav. 60).

The categories of objects on which I intend to focus briefly here can be typologically divided by geographical macro-groups as shown below:

1. pendants from the Adriatic Area (so-called 'Picenians breastplates') (see Fig. 6.5 below);
2. pendants of Dauno-Lucanian type (so-called 'Alianello type') (Fig. 6.6);
3. pendants of Campanian type (Fig. 6.8);
4. anthropomorphic pendants (Southern type) (Fig. 6.9);
5. anthropomorphic pendants (North-central type) (Fig. 6.10).

Despite their apparent heterogeneity, there were several aspects that unite these finds, both from a functional and iconographic point of view. In fact, in all cases they are bronze pendants characterized by the presence of more-or-less evident ornithomorphic elements, in some cases associated with plastic or engraved solar symbols. At least in the first three types this composition recreated the famous archetypal motif – documented since ancient times both in the Mediterranean and in Central Europe – of the so-called 'solar boat' pulled by more or less stylized water birds, in the characteristic form known in German as *vogelsonnenbarke* (Matthäus 1980; 1981: Czyborra 1997; Wirth 2006).

This subject, witnessed in some regions even before the Bronze Age and in an area extended from central-eastern Europe to Egypt and from Asia Minor to Italy, had enormous fortune on the one hand due to the undoubted sacral value which archetypically characterizes the 'sun' and the theme of the 'transition of the sun' and on the other hand for the expressive simplicity and universal comprehensibility of the iconography, figuratively translated into elementary geometric shapes.

The reproduction of the subject over a long period of time, a vast territory and in an infinite variety of objects and materials, determined, independently in different places and periods, various 'deconstructions', 'reinterpretations' or further 'abstractions' of the originals geometrics motifs. These were recombined, redistributed and remixed from time to time in such a way as to lose, in fact or in appearance, their original meaning or, very often, to acquire new ones. The ornithomorphic motif was particularly successful and soon began to be reproduced individually, in a more-or-less stylized form, apparently in autonomy from the solar symbol (which could still be more or less implied), until it became one of the key motifs of the Halstatt and Villanovan geometric figurative tradition (Iaia 2004; Di Fraia 2010; Bettelli 2012; Càssola Guida 2014).

The presumed or real problem of defining the correct iconographic meaning of the pendants in question therefore derives from the difficulty of providing a univocal interpretation of the 'signs' with which they are actually composed. The schematic nature of the forms is such as to make it possible to fall into the error of misunderstanding, over-estimating or ignoring the exact meaning of individual stylistic features.

In the last two pendants types, indeed, the solar and the ornithomorphic elements are both hybridized in a stylized anthropomorphic figure, devoid of sexual connotations. In these examples the motif of the solar 'bird-boat' no longer seems to be the predominant figurative motif, even if it continues to be echoed. In fact, little by little, the human iconographic component seems to prevail over the astral one and is charged with new possible meanings, through a process of hybridization that is not always clear in all its passages (Fig. 6.3).[6]

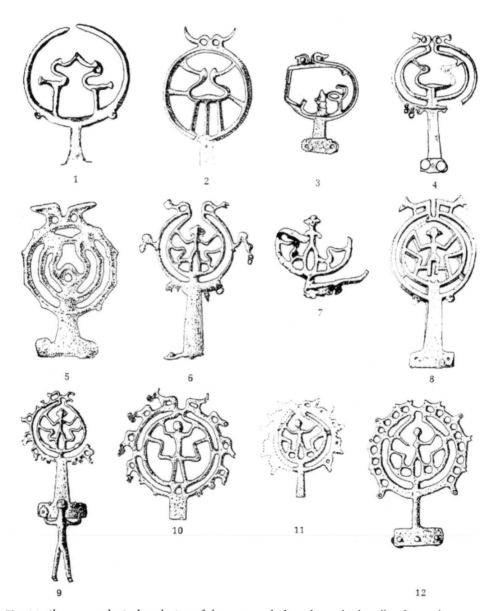

Fig. 6.3: Chrono-typological evolution of the openwork disc above the handle of some bronze cups from Etruria and neighbouring area (from von Merhart 1969, fig. 3).

To put the question on a more solid basis, however, it was necessary to overcome some comparative excesses which uncritically tended to assimilate together objects without real connections both from a cultural, symbolic and figurative point of view (see for example Rossi 2005). The systematic analysis of the principal figurative aspects allowed me to deepen the conceptual and symbolic similarities and differences between the various categories of pendants mentioned and to try to investigate their possible origin and meaning. Moreover, I tried to trace their development thanks to the observation of the way in which the astral appearance of the most ancient specimens had assumed, over time, an anthropomorphic connotation.

In some geographical areas, indeed, the solar disc had been progressively replaced by an anthropomorphic figure placed in the centre of the boat pulled by birds, as in the jewel shown on Figure 6.1 (Cerchiai 2002; Nizzo 2007, 335–336, 351, n. 36 with ref.). As others before me have already tried to hypothesize, behind this last iconography we can perhaps recognize the image of the *Potnia theron*. In this regard, some important observations were developed in the 1990s by the Danish scholar Damgard Andersen without, however, taking into account the amount of evidence considered here, especially the oldest examples (Damgaard Andersen 1996).

The iconography of the *Potnia* is well documented with different variations[7] from the Bronze Age onwards in the Near East and in the Aegean area (Laffineur and Hägg 2001; Babbi 2008b, 320–328; Camporeale 2017). The goddess was depicted in the act of dominating wild animals of various kinds, most commonly birds in the so-called scheme of the *Taubengöttin*. A less common male version depicted a man dominating horses, the so-called *Despotes hippon* (Counts and Arnold 2010; Camporeale 2013; 2016).

These iconographic models began to spread in the indigenous contexts of peninsular Italy only from the mid-8th century BCE and during the Orientalizing period (Guggisberg 2010; Camporeale 2014; 2015). The documentation seems to show how in several cases the iconography of the *Potnia theron* (and perhaps also that of the *Despotes hippon*) overlapped and, over time, replaced that of the solar boat of Central European origin, supplanting the original solar motif with an anthropomorphic subject (Nizzo 2007; Marzatico 2011).

The hybridization between the two motifs and their difficult combination emerges clearly from the way the ornithomorphic elements are treated. In some cases, they are combined with the anthropomorphic figure creating a hybrid between the solar boat and the image of the goddess, who affirms her dominion over nature by taking birds by the neck. In other cases, this result is achieved by combining the silhouette of the arms with that of the birds, giving life to a hybrid figure whose interpretation is still controversial today.

The final result suggests that the craftsmen do not fully understand the original meaning of these representations. The level of stylization and the distance from the prototype suggest that this awareness has been lost over time; nowadays amulets or symbolic objects might no longer faithfully reproduce the iconographic model that inspired them in the past. In my opinion, objects like these can be a fundamental key to understanding the dynamics of contact between the indigenous world and Eastern and Greek immigrants in the crossroads of Western history during the second half of the 8th century.

These influences contributed to the development of new forms of social organization such as cities and to an unavoidable acceleration of identity processes, culminating in an even more complete definition of the ethnic identities of the protohistoric populations of the Italian peninsula. This process was certainly also characterized by important forms of resistance and negotiation of cultural models and, therefore, also of 'images' coming from outside. The pendants in question offer a vivid testimony of these processes, still to be explored.

The power of the sun

The first to deal systematically with these issues was Georg Kossack in a pioneering study which, among his many merits, has that of having shifted attention from the Near East to Central Europe (Kossack 1954; *cf.* more recently 1999). In his research, Kossack undoubtedly contributed to overcoming the well-known *ex oriente lux* paradigm, tackling the examination of the figurative documentation of Central European protohistory with a better method than in the past.

His approach shows in some cases the limits of comparativism. However, Kossack's work has been able to bring attention to a class of objects with high symbolic values but which are not always easy to interpret due to their high schematization. In fact, in the majority of cases these are pendants or, in any case, ornaments created to be worn. The lack of information on the contexts of origin, on the circumstances of the discovery and, therefore, also on the way in which they were used, has undoubtedly made their interpretation more difficult.

Their positioning must have influenced both their shape and their iconography. Objects made to 'dialogue' with the body of the person wearing them had to be imagined as conveying a certain message (on this topic in general *cf.* the various contributions collected in Negroni Catacchio 2016). This visibility could also take on sacral and/or religious values. Objects like these could, in fact, take on amuletic functions, in an apotropaic or auspicious key.

The sun as a symbol of vitality, generation and regeneration is a clear clue to this (Colonna 2007). In the same way, the solar boat alludes to the daily transition of the sun on which the alternation between day and night and the cycle of the seasons depends, which are a guarantee of fertility and, above all, of continuity for societies that depended totally on agriculture for their survival. Finally, it is easy to understand the connection between the fertility of the fields and that of women and men; it explains why pendants, even very voluminous ones, were important ornaments, especially on socially fundamental occasions such as weddings or funerals. Their ostentation could favour their imitation and circulation, also facilitating their more-or-less free re-interpretation, under the influence of external models.

I believe that this could have happened due to the 'contamination' between the 'indigenous' motif of the solar boat and the alien motif of the 'Lady of the animals', even in its masculine variant of the 'Master of the animals'. This contamination was undoubtedly the subject of a slow process of symbolic negotiation which over time has seen the most powerful anthropomorphized allogenic model affirm itself even in the indigenous world. It was therefore not a question of a passive reception imposed from the outside but a choice that involved a more-or-less slow process of assimilation of the alien iconographic component, adapted to the expressive language of indigenous peoples.

These circumstances occur both for simple objects such as pendants and for more complex products of Villanovan metalwork such as the famous bronze ceremonial 'wagon' found in tomb 2 of the Olmo Bello necropolis in Bisenzio, thought to be a censer and/or offering trolley, and the equally extraordinary bronze situla of tomb 25 of the same necropolis, both exhibited in the Museum of Villa Giulia and dating back to ca. 730 BCE. These vases reflect in an extraordinarily expressive way that brief transitional phase between the dominant geometric imagery in the early Iron Age and the first reception of Greek and Oriental models which, in the Orientalizing period, would have led to the definitive affirmation of the Greek mythical model with anthropomorphic divinities (Pacciarelli 2002).

Some iconographic and ritual over-interpretations

In the 1970s, thanks to the research of the Croatian archaeologist Šime Batović (1927–2016), the belief spread that some of the bronze pendants discussed here were inspired by similar Balkan specimens (Batovič 1973; 1975; 1976; 1983; see lastly on these issues with accurate discussion, Blečić-Kavur 2009; Preložnik 2021; Figs 6.4 and 6.11 (1–2)). Batović's dissemination skills had greatly influenced the spread of this belief.[8] His theses were also not easy to deny due to the absence of established chronological contexts, on the basis of which it was possible to define an exact diachronic map of the diffusion of these products. Other difficulties were posed by the simplicity of the representations whose similarity could not even depend on direct influences or processes of imitation.

The ways of reproducing the solar disc or the human figure in abstract and stylized form are necessarily similar in many cultures and in every age.[9] For these reasons it is not always legitimate to establish direct comparisons between realities that may have independently developed similar products. The simplicity of the forms means that some of the Italian anthropomorphic bronzes in question (see above), for some apparent analogies with those widespread in the Balkan and Macedonian areas, have also been interpreted as symbolic axes (Nizzo 2007, 337, 352–353 n. 55). That of the symbolic axes (also in the 'double-axe' version, known in the Aegean worls as *pèlekys*) is a subject with a long tradition (Nizzo 2008, 175–176), widely spread in the

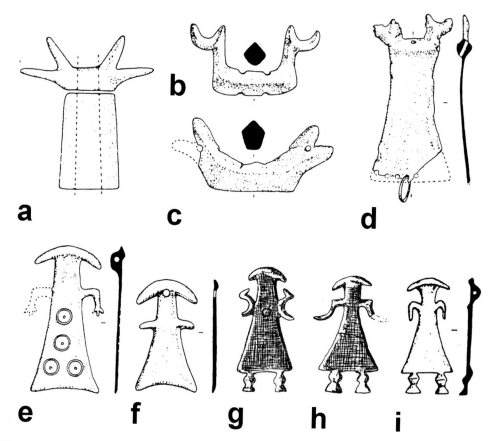

Fig. 6.4: Various types of anthropomorphic pendants from the Iliric area: a–d) Nin; e–f) Zaton; g–h) Smiljan; i) Prozor. Not to scale (from Nizzo 2007, 334, fig. 6, with ref.).

Aegean world since the Bronze Age but which, in my opinion, has little to do with the pendants discussed here. I will return to this issue shortly.

Another recurrent interpretative error derives from the identification as praying people or mourning women of some anthropomorphic pendants found in funerary contexts in the Dauno-Lucanian area (Nizzo 2007, 335–336 with ref.). However, this possibility should be excluded because the funerary connotation of the context has little to do with the daily use of objects that had to be regularly worn before ending up in a tomb. This is clearly demonstrated by the traces of deterioration produced by their rubbing on the body and by the discovery of some pendants in sanctuaries, in which they most likely had to be consecrated together with the clothes on which they were worn.

There is no possible funerary characterization of their iconography, although some scholars have hypothesized this by interpreting the ornithomorphic arms facing upwards as the well-known attitude of weeping women – an interpretative short-circuit due to the lack of information on the funerary contexts in which many have been found.

Another important aspect is linked to the possibility that objects like these, given their symbolic meaning, could be 'handed-down' together with parade dresses or, for example, wedding dresses even for several generations, before ending their journey in a tomb. Their 'biography' could therefore have been much longer than what is usually imagined. This aspect can affect their dating and only future discoveries may allow us to solve the many aspects that are still problematic today.

As previously anticipated, let us now pass quickly to examine the main types of bronze pendants on which it is appropriate to focus attention for the purposes of this work.

Solar boat pendants with bird protomes

The first nucleus of objects to be considered is made up of bronze plates in the shape of a more or less stylized solar boat, composed of one or more elements connected together by chains, with further chains and/or pendants suspended from their terminals. These plates were worn with different methods of suspension at the height of the chest or, more frequently, of the belly. In the few cases in which we have information about the circumstances of their discovery, these pendants were always worn by female individuals.

Pendants from the Adriatic area (so-called 'Picenians breastplates')

Figure 6.5 shows some characteristic breastplates of the Piceno area documented from the first half of the 8th century BCE. Their diffusion affects both sides of the Adriatic (Hiller 2001; Nizzo 2007, 341–344, cat. 228–229, 355, nn. 78–80; Kukoč 2016), with variants of different complexity summarized in this figure. The solar boat motif is easily recognizable although in some specimens it is taken to the highest level of abstraction. The disc of the sun could also be represented with a decoration engraved on the slab, with motifs in circles, crosses or swastikas. Engraved motifs and chains could recall the sun's rays, which could be also emphasized by means of glass paste beads. The original golden colour of bronze made the overall effect even more evocative. The set of chains and pendants also produced acoustic effects once worn, perhaps able to evoke the rustle of the sea waves on which the solar boat ideally made its daily journey.

The interpretation of these pendants as 'breastplates' is not always correct (Nizzo 2007, 347, nn. 6–7). When the circumstances of the discovery became known, it was realized that they could be suspended not only on the chest but, above all, in the belly area. This is a significant aspect if we consider that a few well-known grave goods all refer to dead females.

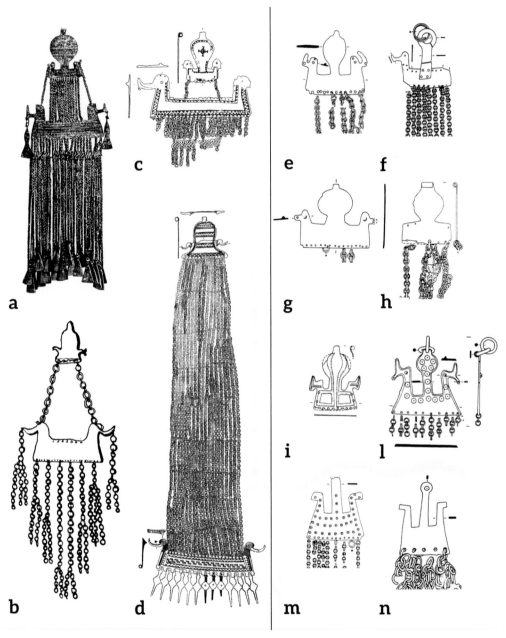

Fig. 6.5: Solar boat pendants from the Adriatic area. With 'double' plate: a) Monteprandone; b) Ancona, Colle Cardeto; c) Acquaviva Picena; d) Zaton, t. 6. With 'single' plate: e–i) Novilara Servici: t. 32; t. 85; t. 92; t. 93; no context; l–n) Novilara Molaroni, t. 135; t. 78; t. 36. Not to scale (adapted from Nizzo 2007, 331, figs 1–2, with ref).

The plaque could, therefore, coincide with the genital area and this circumstance, if we consider the connection previously mentioned with the regenerative faculties of the sun, should not have been accidental.[10] The coincidence with the female genitals can therefore allude to the generative power of the woman who, also through the use of ornaments like these, could be placed under the protection of the sun, guarantor of the fertility of the earth and of men.The presence of solar motifs engraved on the characteristic Villanovan lozenge belts probably starts from the same conceptual assumptions and highlights a common cultural matrix, albeit expressed through different objects and ornaments (most recently Naso 2020, with ref.).

To increase their visual impact, these pendants could be divided into several plates, joined by chains. The size and length could thus also vary in a very significant way, as evidenced by extraordinary specimens such as that from Canavaccio di Urbino (excavations 1928; D.G. Lollini in Percossi Serenelli 1998, 51, tav. II), found in a context in which the pendant was associated with precious amber ornaments, as documented in several other burials. As is well known, amber is also associated with the sun (Nava and Salerno 2007; Negroni Catacchio 2011; Causey 2011). Its mythical origins led back to the tears of the Electrides, the sisters of Phaeton son of the sun, who died near the Po delta after stealing their father's chariot. The Po was a fundamental communication and trade route towards Central Europe and the emphasis placed in the Adriatic area on amber objects and iconographic and mythical motifs connected to the sun does not seem casual.

If we consider that some of these plaques dates back at least to the first half of the 8th century BCE, it is evident that we are dealing with an iconographic model of high antiquity and relevance that precedes the diffusion of anthropomorphic motifs related to the solar boat. In the most recent examples, the stylization almost completely cancels the recognizability of the *vogelsonnenbarke* motif. The water birds disappear completely and the composition takes on geometric characters very far from the most ancient prototypes. This circumstance is perhaps an indication that both the artisans and the users may have now forgotten the original meaning of the iconography of these pendants.

Pendants of Dauno-Lucanian type (so-called 'Alianello type')
The so-called Dauno-Lucanian pendants (or 'Alianello', from one of the archaeological sites in Basilicata region where they were found: Nizzo 2007, 331–333, 337–338, 348, nn. 9–11) are very similar to the Picenean breastplates? (Fig. 6.6). Their dating is more recent. In fact, the attestations are concentrated in the 7th and 6th centuries BCE and this could also justify their high stylization.

Context data offers valuable insights into how they were worn. The plate in the shape of a solar boat was suspended from a belt consisting of the intertwining of several chains. In this type, the plate also coincided with the female genital area. In some cases, the solar disc could be symbolized by a circular pendant also connected to

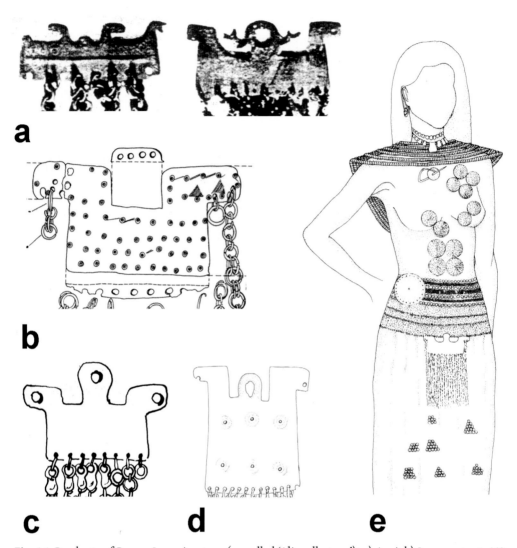

Fig. 6.6: Pendants of Dauno-Lucanian type (so-called 'Alianello type'): a) Anzi; b) Incoronata, t. 468; c) San Chirico Nuovo; d) Crotone, Santuario di Hera Lacinia; e) Alianello, t. 316 (riconstruction from d'Agostino 1998, 38, fig. 10). Not to scale (from Nizzo 2007, 332, fig. 2, with ref).

the belt. The composition as a whole recalls the Picenian examples iconographically and functionally. It therefore seems legitimate to hypothesize some reciprocal influence.

The consecration of a pendant in the Greek sanctuary of Hera Lacinia in Capo Colonna suggests the perception of its relevance by whoever dedicated the object as an offering. This might be a votive gift devoted to Hera by a woman of Dauno-Lucanian origin who offered the goddess an object that was particularly dear to her, probably together with the garments – perhaps the wedding ones – with which the object was worn (Spadea 1997; Marino 2008, 67–68, fig. 2).

Finds like these immediately bring to mind the famous epigram in which the Locrian poetess Nossis remembered the peplos consecrated to Hera Lacinia together with her mother (*Anth. Pal.* VI, 265); a typical offering of – Greeks and Indigenous – pilgrims who went to pray at the sanctuary of Croton:

> Ἥρα τιμήεσσα, Λακίνιον ἃ τὸ θυῶδες
> πολλάκις οὐρανόθεν νεισομένα καθορῇς,
> δέξαι βύσσινον εἶμα, τό τοι μετὰ παιδὸς ἀγαυᾶς
> Νοσσίδος ὕφανεν Θευφιλὶς ἀ Κλεόχας.

> Hera revered, who oft descending from heaven
> lookest on thy Lacinian shrine fragrant with frankincense,
> accept the linen garment which Theophilis, daughter of Cleocha,
> wove for thee with her noble daughter Nossis (transl. W.R. Paton, The Greek Anthology.
> Vol. 1. London, The Loeb Classical Library, 1952 [1916], p. 441).

A daunian olla from Ferrandina, t. 5 (early 7th century BCE) most likely reproduces one of these pendants (Adamesteanu 1971, 29, tav. vi: Fig. 6.7a, notice a small swastika on both sides). A double plate pendant, with a circular element probably alluding to the sun, appears on a typical daunian stele (Nava 1988, 11, 195, fig. 214: Fig. 6.7b) and in this case the functional and conceptual similarity with the Piceno specimens is evident. The stele is in turn a stylized reproduction of the human body, so it is not always easy to obtain precise information about the pendent position on the body, but its meaning is fairly well understood.

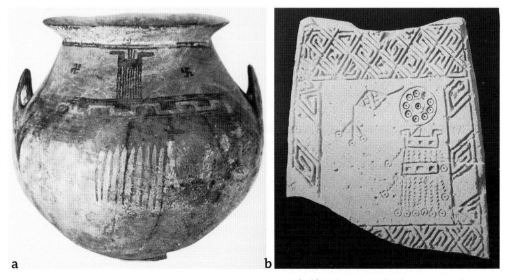

a   b

Fig. 6.7: *Pendants of Dauno-Lucanian type reproduced on (left) a daunian olla from Ferrandina, t. 5 (from Adamesteanu 1971, tav. VI) and (right) on a daunian stele (from Nava 1988, 195, fig. 214).*

Pendants of Campanian type

With this type we returned to Campania, where we initially started. Figure 6.8 collected some of the most characteristic pendants found in the Villanovan and indigenous contexts of the region, together with some extraordinary parade fibulae which were sometimes associated in some of the richest tombs of the necropolis of Capua (Nizzo 2007, 333–335, 344–345, cat. 230, 349–350, nn. 2--25; 2020c).

We owe the excavation of some of the contexts to Werner Johannowsky (see also Melandri 2011, 353, type 139J). These authors have helped us understand the association of pendants with fibulae of this type. We are in the second half of the 8th century and on the parade fibula (Fig. 6.8d) can be seen, together with a bull, a series of ornithomorphic protomes and the motif of the man in the centre of a solar boat that we first saw in the jewels of Nunzia Laura Saldalamacchia (Fig. 6.1 above). The anthropomorphic component appears for the first time in these specimens and, as mentioned, it seems to take the place of the solar disc.

On the other hand, in this kind of ornaments we can recognize – albeit in stylized form – some of the elements observed in the Piceno and Dauno-Lucanian specimens. The motif of the solar boat is barely recognizable in the horizontal plate. The grid elements that join the ring to the plate seem to recall the rays of the sun, forming an original composition, in which the ornithomorphic component survives in the small apophyses or in pendants suspended from the triangular slab. In other specimens, stylized anthropomorphic pendants appear instead of birds.

The provenance of objects with such particular iconographies, from places subjected to a more or less direct Villanovan political and cultural influence, such as Capua and Suessula or from the indigenous settlement of Cuma, may have been favoured by early contacts with the Greek and Eastern world following the first Hellenic *apoikia* of Pithekoussai on the Ischia island in the first half of the 8th century BCE. The development of Campanian bronze figurative plastic was almost certainly encouraged by the increasing relationship with the first Euboic settlers and it is probably also thanks to their influence that we have exploits such as the Capuan parade fibulas, the famous Lucera's *Kesselwagen* or the similar specimen – without context but certainly Campanian – in the National Archaeological Museum of Naples (Cerchiai 2002; Nizzo 2007, 333–340; Cerchiai and Salvadori 2012, 443–452; Bonghi Jovino 2016a; Cinquantaquattro and Rescigno 2017, 230; on the Lucera's and Naples' ceremonial wagons see, respectively, Pietropaolo 2002 and Nizzo 2020b). It should therefore not surprise us that a wagon of the Lucera's type was recently identified among the votive offerings consecrated in the sanctuary of Olympia, where several etrusco-italic imports are early documented, as it happens at the same time also in other Greek sacred contexts (Naso 2016, 281–282, fig. 5a–b).

Note how the human figure placed in the centre of the solar boat on parade fibulae or applied to other supports such as the censer lid mentioned at the beginning of this paper is devoid of sexual connotations and in a characteristic attitude, with one hand raised to the head and the other positioned in the pelvic area. Some anthropomorphic representations of this type have a vase-shaped object on the head, reproduced in a more-or-less abstract and stylized form but sufficient to allow an identification of the subject with the archetypical iconographic model of the 'lady at the fountain/ water carrier' (Richardson 1984; Nizzo 2007, 336–337, 351, n. 38, with ref.).

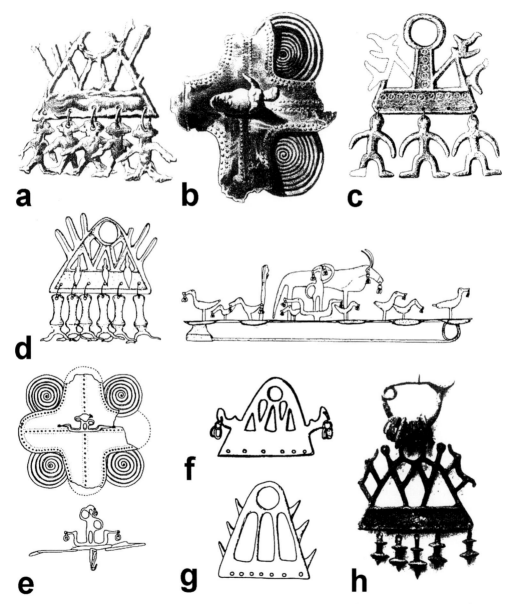

Fig. 6.8: Pendants of Campanian type: a–b, f–g) Suessula; c) Cuma; d–e) Capua, t. 368; t. 363; h) Cuma, collezione Osta. Not to scale (from Nizzo 2007, 333, fig. 4, with ref).

Without going into more detail on this latter interpretation, my idea is that with such specimens we are faced with the first elaboration of an iconographic syncretism between the motif of the solar boat and that of the master/mistress of the animals. The process is at the beginning and the indigenous peoples have not yet fully understood the Hellenic imaginary, with its corollary of myths and anthropomorphic divinities such as Apollo, Athena or Artemis. However, the lack of contexts does not allow us to further investigate these hypotheses or to clarify the possible links and influences with the other cultural spheres mentioned above. Objects like these were often used in the 19th century to compose a pastiche that have almost completely altered their original conformation, as in an example preserved in the British Museum (Aigner Foresti 1986).

Anthropomorphic pendants with bird protomes

In the last pendants discussed I will focus on how the solar boat is incorporated in the stylization of the anthropomorphic figure. The result is that the suspension ring can be identified with both a head and a solar disc and the arms take on the typical sinuosity of ornithomorphic protomes. What appears as a body is a simple elongated trapezoid with no legs or feet to the point that some scholars have interpreted the entire pendant as a miniaturized ax (so-called *beil-anhänger*: see for example Papadopoulos 2003, 68–69; *cf.* also Martelli 2004, 9–10, 21, n. 48).

Anthropomorphic pendants (Southern type)

In one of the specimens of the Gorga Collection (Nizzo 2007, 330–331, 337, 345–347, cat. 233, here Fig. 6.2), the presence underneath the birds/arms of two pendants of the shape of a crouching monkey strengthened my belief that behind these subjects we must recognize the stylized iconography of the *Potnia theron*, syncretistically combined with the simplified motif of the solar boat (most recently Preložnik 2021, 232–236).

The area of diffusion of these specimens is slightly wider than the 'Alianello' type pendants and extends from southern Campania to Daunia and Lucania (Figs 6.9, 6.11 (4)). Despite the lack of contexts, the chronology runs from the end of the 7th through to the entire 6th century BCE. Two fragmentary specimens were found in the Calabrian sanctuary of Athena in Francavilla Marittima (Papadopoulos 2003, 68–69, 175, figs 88a–b; 6.9i–l) and in that of Dodona in Epirus (Kilian-Dirlmeier 1979, 243, tav. 90, n. 1563; Dakaris 1985, 112–113, fig. 2b; Naso 2016, 281–282, n. 26: fig. 9m), a circumstance that confirms, as seen above, their symbolic importance.

Anthropomorphic pendants (North-central type)

The last pendants considered in this paper are similar to the previous ones but their area of diffusion extends from northern Campania to the Po Valley with variants that reach the Alpine area, Central Europe and northern Balkans (Nizzo 2007, 337–340;

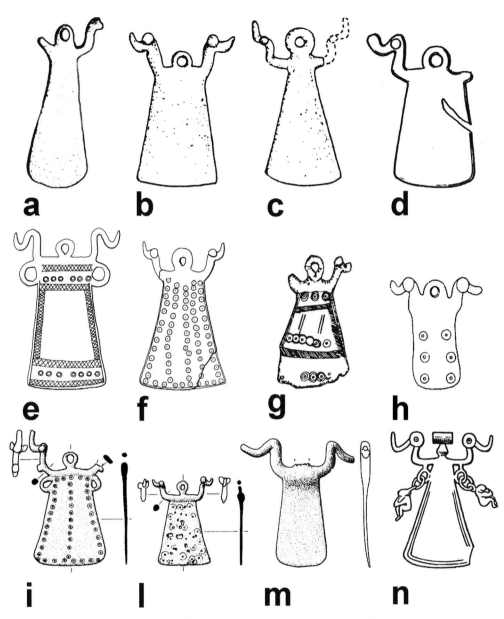

Fig. 6.9: Anthropomorphic pendants (Southern type): a) Ascoli Satriano, collina del Serpente; b) Canne, Pezza la Forbice; c) Monte Saraceno, Collezione Sansone; d) Ruvo, Museo Jatta; e–f) Lavello; g) Ottati, collezione Gatti; h) Roscigno, no context; i–l) Francavilla Marittima, Timpone Motta, Santuario di Atena; m) Dodona, Santuario di Zeus; n) Italy, unknown location. Not to scale (from Nizzo 2007, 335, fig. 7, with ref).

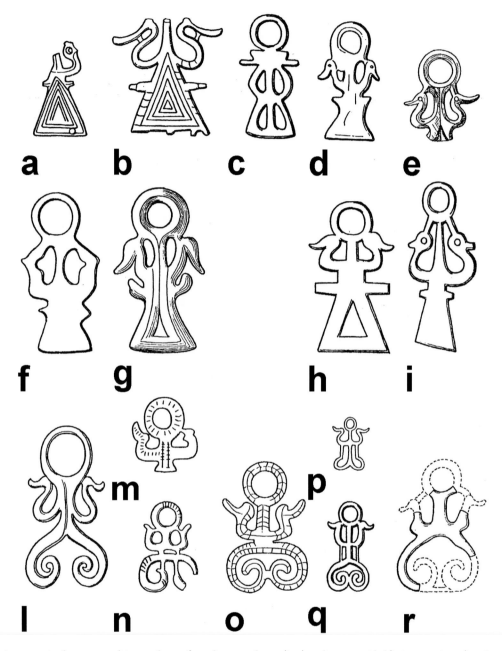

*Fig. 6.10: Anthropomorphic pendants (North-central type): a) Velem St Vid; b) Gorszewice; c) Ca'
Morta (Como); d) Italy, unknown location; e, i, p) Bologna; f) Ossero (Fiume); g) Bisenzio; h) Este; l)
Ramonte (Marzabotto); m–n) Vadena-Pfattenn; o, q) Sanzeno (Trento); r) Frog. Not to scale (from
Nizzo 2007, 335, fig. 8, with ref).*

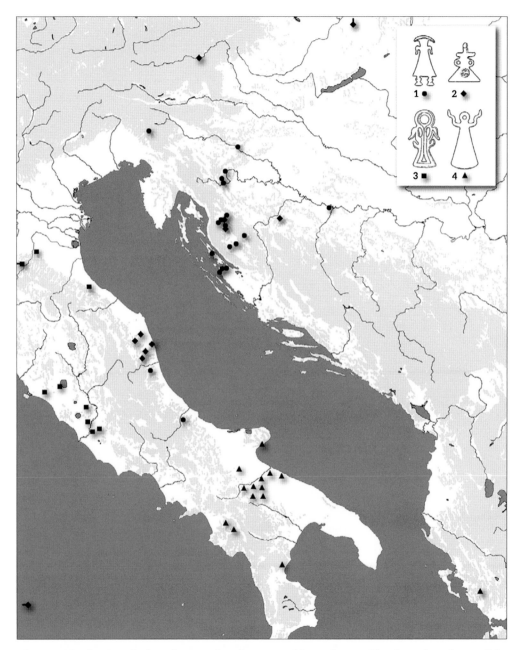

Fig. 6.11: Distribution of selected types of anthropomorphic pendants with triangular scheme of the 7th and 6th centuries BCE: 1) Iapodian anthropomorphic pendants; 2) Picenian-Iapodian type 1 (after Blečić-Kavur 2009, fig. 7); 3) Etruscan type 2a (after Blečić-Kavur 2017, fig. 4); 4) Dauno-Lucanian (after Nizzo 2007, 356, n. 94) (from Preložnik 2021, 234, fig. 8, adapted by the author).

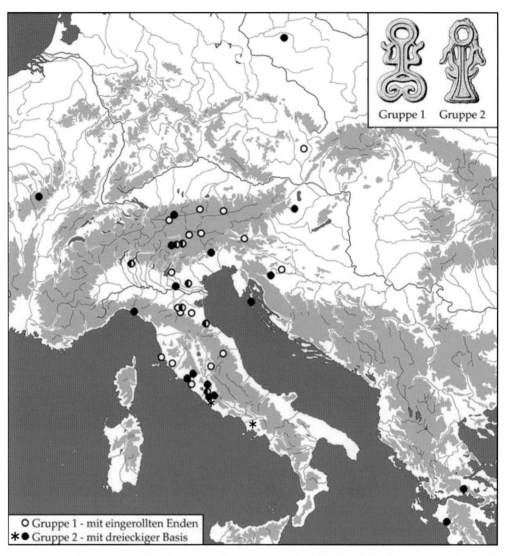

Fig. 6.12: Distribution map of anthropomorphic pendants (North-central type) Group 1: with double spiral base, Group 2: with trapezoidal base (from Kirchmayr 2017, 329, fig. 8 updated by the author with an asterisk).

Blečić-Kavur 2017; Kirchmayr 2017; Preložnik 2021, 232–236; Figs 6.10, 6.11 (3), 6.12). Also in this case some specimens were found in Greek sanctuaries, in Delphi and Olympia (Kilian 1977), where they probably arrived as war plunder since, unlike those listed above, these pendants were not worn but were frequently suspended in pairs at the edge of shields or on the handles of bronze vases. The chronology is older and goes from the mid-8th to mid-7th century BCE, with even more recent variants.

A recent study conducted by M. Kirchmayr has collected a good number of specimens, organized the typology of the main variants (already known since Kossack's studies) and edited a series of updated maps of their distribution (Kirchmayr 2017; see here Fig. 6.12).[11] The two most common variants differ in the shape of the base: either double spiral or trapezoid. As in the Southern examples, the element that most characterizes them is the symbiosis between the motif of the solar boat and the anthropomorphic one. Their recurrence in high-ranking grave goods shows that they were not common objects. The association with products of high metallurgical craftsmanship has undoubtedly facilitated their geographical spread also through the commercial circuit of the aristocratic gift.

Their suspension on the shields in associated pairs along the flat side presumably indicates an acoustic function, perhaps associated with the practice of warrior dances which involved the use of shields as percussion instruments in rituals such as those practised by the Salii priests with the their bilobed shields: the anciles (Nizzo 2018, 103, n. 39 with ref.). The conformation of the arms as ornithomorphic or equine protomes seems to also confirm their inspiration from the motif of the *Potnia theron* or that of the *Despotes hippon*.

The possession of war chariots and horses is one of the most predominant status symbols among the princes/warriors of the second half of the 8th century, as showed by the recurrence of elements of the equine harness and the spread of the horse master motif also on ceramics (Camporeale 2004–2005; 2013; 2015; 2016; 2017).

Final remarks

With this quick analysis I have tried to show a series of cultural processes that move in parallel and almost simultaneously in several distinct topographical areas and which are united by the assimilation of the anthropomorphic component to solar motifs of an older tradition. In areas such as Piceno, the pendants maintain their original astral connotation, simplifying it until it is no longer understandable. At the same time, in the Orientalizing period and during the 7th century, the assimilation of Near Eastern and Greek mythical and iconographic models begins to be more and more complete, favoured by the filter of hybrid figures such as *Potnia theron* and the *Despotes hippon* whose generic figurative connotation undoubtedly helped to facilitate this transition. As early as the mid-7th century, the remains of the oldest indigenous iconographic repertoire now appear almost completely contaminated by the contribution of external models. Their original meaning was perhaps no longer understandable even to those who wore objects of this type every day during the 6th century BCE. At that time Apollo, Poseidon, Athena, Artemis and the other gods of Olympus settled at the expense of those archetypal mythical figures such as *Potnia theron* and the *Despotes hippon*, who have now also become the legacy of a more-or-less remote religious and forgotten feeling.

Notes

1 *Potnia theron*, the lady of the animals, as defined by Homer (Iliad, book XXI, v. 470) with reference to Artemis.
2 On the 'multiform' concept of 'agency' in the archaeological field cf. Dobres and Robb (2000); Hodder (2000); Barrett (2001); Dornan (2002); Hodder and Hutson (2003, 99ff); Hodder (2004, 31–34); and, in critical terms, Trigger (2007, 469–470); for a picture of the last implications of theoretical reflection on the relationship between 'agency' and 'material culture' and on the concept of social life of things see also Nizzo (2015, 204–211, 224–232, 460–463, 474–478 with references and *ad ind. s. v.* 'agency'.
3 < https://www.archeostorie.it/nymphe-archeologia-gioielli/ > (*vidi* 26/3/2022).
4 On this class of object in general, see Horsnaes (2001, 18, fig. 7 and *passim*). On its ritual significance see Iaia (2005, 211, with refs).
5 In general, about the Gorga's Collection see Capodiferro (2013).
6 See, for example, the chrono-typological evolution of the openwork disc above the handle of some bronze cups from Etruria and neighbouring areas carefully examined by Gero von Merhart, who collocated the type with birds at the beginning of the developing process, and the one with the human figurine at the end: von Merhart (1969, 273–279, fig. 3; see also Camporeale 2004–2005; Babbi 2008b).
7 Included the ancient Near Eastern archetypical iconography of the naked female figure between lotus flowers: Delpino (2006); Babbi (2008a).
8 Among Italian scholars, despite a general (and in some cases generic) adhesion to Batovič's theories, there was no lack of important synthesis works, with often critical or more articulated conclusions on the interpretation of the phenomenon of inter-Adriatic relations: *cf.* in particular Lo Schiavo (1970; 1984) and Peroni (1976). More recently, on the relations between Piceno and Illyrian, see Lucentini (2001) and D'Ercole (2002).
9 For the evolution of human iconography in protohistoric Europe see, in general, Huth (2003), Babbi (2008b) and Rebay-Salisbury (2016, 108–251).
10 Note how the same possible symbolic meaning can also be attributed to the bronze discs with geometric decoration produced between the 8th and 6th centuries BCE among the peoples of the Central Apennines whose belonging to the female costume has recently been demonstrated, allowing us to reject the often proposed hypothesis of their use as armour discs (Colonna 2007, 17–22). As Colonna brilliantly demonstrated, the most usual practice was to apply one relatively large and one smaller disc to the opposite ends of a stole worn hanging from the neck, so that the larger disc hung over the breast and the smaller fell over the pubis. The discs not only alluded to the primary function of the woman in terms of continuation of the line but also associated her with the sun cult, recorded among the Sabines and Marsi, as also in proto-historical Hallstattian and Scandinavian cultures.
11 To the specimens collected by Kirchmayr must be added at least the pendants of the type with a trapezoid base (*Gruppe 2 - mit dreieckiger Basis*) associated in pairs with the round Villanovan bronze shields of tomb 21 at Castel di Decima, Rome (Nizzo 2018, 103, n. 39) and those suspended from the handles of the bronze olla of tomb 285 from Calatia, Naples (Nizzo 2020d), shown here on the distribution map (Fig. 6.13) with an asterisk.

References

Adamesteanu, D. (1971) Ferrandina. In *Popoli anellenici in Basilicata*, 27–29. Napoli, La buona stampa.
Aigner Foresti, L. (1986) Su un arredo della Campania. In J. Swaddling (ed.) *Italian Iron Age Artefacts in the British Museum, Papers of the Sixth British Museum Classical Colloquium*, 37–41. London, British Museum Publications.

Babbi, A. (2008a) Iconographic traditions of the Hittite and Syrian 'sich entschleiernde Göttin' and the Egyptian and Syrian–Palestinian 'Qu-du-shu' in the central-Tyrrhenian area from the 9th to the 7th century B.C. In M. Harari, S. Paltineri and M. T. A. Robino (eds) *Icone del mondo antico. Un seminario di storia delle immagini. Pavia 25 novembre 2005*, 13–29. Rome, Studia Archaeologica 167.

Babbi, A. (2008b) *La piccola plastica fittile antropomorfa dell'Italia antica. Dal Bronzo finale all'Orientalizzante. Mediterranea*, Supplement 1. Pisa–Roma, Serra.

Barrett, J. C. (2001) Agency: A Revisionist Account. In I. Hodder (ed.), *Archaeological Theory Today*, Second edition, 146-166. Cambridge, Polity Press.

Batovič, Š. (1973) Nin e l'Italia Meridionale nell'età del ferro. *Archivio storico pugliese* 26, 389–421.

Batovič, Š. (1975) Le relazioni tra la Daunia e le sponde orientali dell'Adriatico. In *Preistoria e protostoria della Daunia. Atti del Colloquio Internazionale Foggia, 24-29 Aprile 1973*, 149–157. Firenze, Istituto Italiano di Preistoria e Protostoria.

Batovič, Š. (1976) Le relazioni culturali tra le sponde adriatiche nell'età del ferro. In *Jadranska Obala u Protohistoriji Kulturni i etnicki problemi. Simpozij Odrzan o Dubrovniku 19-23 ottobre 1972*, 11–93. Zagreb, Liber.

Batovič, Š. (1983) Problemes de l'age du Fer dans la region Balkano–Adriatique. In *L'Adriatico tra Mediterraneo e penisola balcanica nell'antichità* (Lecce-Matera, 21–27 ottobre 1973), 67–85. Taranto, Istituto per la storia e l'archeologia della Magna Grecia.

Bettelli, M. (2012) Variazioni sul sole: immagini e immaginari nell'Europa protostorica. *Studi Micenei ed Egeo-Anatolici* 54, 185–205.

Blečić-Kavur, M. (2009) Japodske podlaktične narukvice: simbolika ženskog principa u optjecanju ideja i djela jadranske kulturne koine. *Vjesnik Arheološkog muzeja u Zagrebu* 3 series 42, 231–258.

Blečić-Kavur, M. (2017) Mala tijela u velikom svijetu: antropo-ornitomorfni privjesci željeznog doba Caput Adriae/Small bodies in a big world: anthropo-ornithomorphic Iron Age pendants from Caput Adriae. *Prilozi Instituta za arheologiju u Zagrebu* 34, 123–142.

Bonghi Jovino, M. (2016) Per gli uomini e per gli dei. Simbolismo e significazione. Una fibula da parata della necropoli capuana. In Negroni Catacchio 2016, vol. 2, 529–556.

Camporeale, G. (2004–2005) Cavalli e Cavalieri nell'Etruria dell'VIII sec. a.C. Dall'Agro falisco all'Agro picentino. *Rendiconti della Pontificia Accademia di Archeologia* 77, 381–411.

Camporeale, G. (2013) Cacciatore e Despotes Theron su un elmo fittile da Pontecagnano. *Studi Etruschi* 76, 3–10.

Camporeale, G. (2014) Medusa-Potnia Theron nella produzione etrusca dell'Orientalizzante dell'arcaismo. In S. Bruni, L. Donati (eds) *Lautus erat tuscis Porsena fictilibus. Studi e ricerche sul bucchero dell'area chiusina per Luigi Donati*, 247–264. Pisa, ETS.

Camporeale, G. (2015) Potnia e Despotes Theron nelle oreficerie vetuloniesi di età orientalizzante. *Studi Etruschi* 78, 21–32.

Camporeale, G. (2016) Il despotes theron nella ceramica tardo-villanoviana e orientalizzante di Narce e Capena. In M.C. Biella and E. Giovannelli (eds) *Nuovi studi sul bestiario fantastico di età orientalizzante nella penisola italiana*, 63–84. Trento, Tangram Edizioni Scientifiche.

Camporeale, G. (2017) Genesi, sviluppo, senso di un motivo figurativo di età villanoviana. La potnia (e il despotes) theron. In L. Cappuccini, C. Leypold and M. Mohr, *Fragmenta Mediterranea. Contatti, tradizioni e innovazioni in Grecia, Magna Grecia, Etruria e Roma. Studi in onore di Christoph Reusser*, 251–261. Sesto Fiorentino, All'Insegna del Giglio.

Capodiferro, A. ed. (2013) *Evan Gorga la collezione di archeologia, Museo Nazionale Romano*. Milano, Electa.

Càssola Guida, P. (2014) Tra cielo e mare: ancora qualche nota sull'iconografia del viaggio del sole. In M. Chiabà (ed.) *HOC QVOQVE LABORIS PRAEMIVM. Scritti in onore di Gino Bandelli*, 33–52. Trieste, EUT – Edizioni Università di Trieste.

Causey, F. (2011) *Amber and the Ancient World*, Los Angeles CA, J. Paul Getty Museum.

Cerchiai, L. (2002) Le fibule da parata di Capua e Suessula. In Pietropaolo 2002, 143–147.

Cerchiai, L. and Salvadori, Y. (2012) La tomba 39 di via San Massimo a Nola. Breve spunto per la cronologia dell'inizio dell'insediamento proto–urbano. In C. Chiaramonte Treré, G. Bagnasco Gianni and F. Chiesa (eds) *Interpretando l'antico: scritti di archeologia offerti a Maria Bonghi Jovino* vol. 1, 435–455. Milano, Quaderni di 'Acme' 134.

Cinquantaquattro, T.E. and Rescigno, C. (2017) Una suonatrice di lira e un guerriero. Due bronzetti dagli scavi sull'acropoli di Cuma. *Mélanges de l'École Française de Rome* 129 (1), 217–234.

Colonna, G. (2007), Dischi-corazza e dischi di ornamento femminile: due distinte classi di bronzi centro–italici. *Archeologia Classica* 58, 3–30.

Counts, D.B. and Arnold, B. eds (2010) *The Master of Animals in Old World Iconography*. Budapest, Archaeolingua Alapítvány.

Czyborra, I. (1997) Eisenzeitliche Vogeldarstellungen im ägäisch–adriatischen Raum, in C. Becker (ed.) Χρονος. *Beiträge zur prähistorischen Archäologie zwischen Nord- und Südosteuropa. Festschrift für Bernhard Hänsel*, 619–626. Espelkamp, Leidorf.

d'Agostino, B. (1998) Greci e indigeni in Basilicata dall'VIII al III secolo a.C. In *Tesori dell'Italia del Sud. Greci e Indigeni in Basilicata, Catalogo della mostra, Strasburgo 1998*, 24–57. Ginevra-Milano, Skira.

D'Ercole, M.C. (2002) *Importuosa Italiae litora. Paysage et échanges dans l'Adriatique méridionale et archaïque*. Naples, Centre Jean Bérard.

Dakaris, S.I. (1985), Epiro e Magna Grecia fino all'età arcaica. In *Magna Grecia, Epiro e macedonia, Atti del XXIV Convegno di studi sulla Magna Grecia (Taranto 1984)*, 103–131. Napoli, Istituto per la Storia e l'Archeologia della Magna Grecia.

Damgaard Andersen, H. (1996) The origin of Potnia Theron in central Italy. In *Die Akten des Internationalen Kolloquiums 'Interactions in the Iron Age: Phoenicians, Greeks, and the Indigenous Peoples of the Western Mediterranean', Amsterdam am 26. und 27. März 1992*, 73–113. *Hamburger Beiträge zur Archäologie 19–20*.

Delpino, F. (2006) Una identità ambigua. Figurette femminili nude di area etrusco–italica. Congiunte, antenate o divinità? *Mediterranea* 3, 33–54.

Di Fraia, T. (2010) Immagini ornitomorfe e motivi solari nel Bronzo Recente e Finale in Italia. In *Imaginer et représenter l'au-delà. Actes du 132e Congrès national des sociétés historiques et scientifiques, « Images et imagerie »*, Arles 2007, 7–22. Paris, Editions du CTHS.

Dobres, M. and Robb, J. eds (2000) *Agency in Archaeology*. London, Cambridge University Press.

Dornan, J. L. (2002) Agency and Archaeology: Past, Present, and Future Directions. In *Journal of Archaeological Method and Theory* 9, 303–329.

Guggisberg, M.A. (2010) The mistress of animals, the master of animals. Two complementary or oppositional religious concepts in early Celtic art? In Counts and Arnold 2010, 223–236.

Hiller, G. (2001) Vogelbarkenpektorale vom picenisch-liburnischen Typ. In R.M. Boehmer and J. Maran (eds) *Lux Orientis. Archäologie zwischen Asien und Europa. Festschrift für Harald Hauptmann zum 65. Geburtstag*, 197–200. Rahden, Leidorf.

Hodder, I. (1982) Theoretical archaeology: a reactionary view. In I. Hodder (ed.) *Symbolic and Structural Archaeology*, 1–16. Cambridge, Cambridge University Press.

Hodder, I. (2000) Agency and individuals in long-term processes, in Dobres and Robb 2000, 21–33.

Hodder, I. (2004) The 'Social' in Archaeological Theory: An Historical and Contemporary Perspective, in L. M. Meskell and R. W. Preucel (eds.), *A companion to social archaeology*, 23–42. Malden, Blackwell Publishing.

Hodder, I. and Hutson, S. eds (2003 [1986]) *Reading the past. Current approaches to interpretation in archaeology*, 3rd ed. Cambridge, Cambridge University Press.

Horsnaes, H.W. (2001) A Villanovan «Censer» from Pontecagnano in the Danish National Museum. *Analecta Romana Instituti Danici* 27, 7–36.

Huth, C. (2003) *Menschenbilder und Menschenbild: anthropomorphe Bildwerke der frühen Eisenzeit*. Berlin, Reimer.

Iaia, C. (2004) Lo stile della 'barca solare ornitomorfa' nella toreutica italiana della prima età del ferro. In N. Negroni Catacchio (ed.) *Miti, simboli, decorazioni. Ricerche e scavi, Atti del VI incontro* di Studi 'Preistoria e Protostoria in Etruria' (Pitigliano, Valentano, settembre 2002), 307–318. Milano, Centro Studi di Preistoria e Archeologia.

Iaia, C. (2005) *Produzioni toreutiche della prima età del Ferro in Italia centro-settentrionale. Stili decorativi, circolazione, significato.* Pisa-Rome, Istituti editoriali e poligrafici internazionali.

Jakobson, R. (1960) Closing statements: linguistics and poetics. In T.A. Sebeok (ed.) *Style in Language,* 350–377. New York, Wiley,

Kilian, K. (1977) Zwei italische Neufunde der Früheisenzeit aus Olympia. *Archäologisches Korrespondenzblatt* 7, 121–126.

Kilian Dirlmeier, I. (1979) *Anhänger in Griechenland von der mykenischen bis zur spätgeometrischen Zeit (Griechisches Festland, Ionische Inseln, dazu Albanien und Jugoslawisch Mazedonien',* Munich, Prähistorische Bronzefunde XI (2).

Kirchmayr, M. (2017) Anthropomorphe Anhänger mit Vogelprotomen – Neue Erkenntnisse zu einem eisenzeitlichen Anhängertyp. *Sonderdruck aus Archäologisches Korrespondenzblatt* 47 (3), 319–339.

Kossack, G. (1954) *Studien zum Symbolgut der Urnenfelder- und Hallstattzeit Mitteleuropas.* Berlin, de Gruyter.

Kossack, G. (1999) *Religiöses Denken in dinglicher und bildlicher Überlieferung Alteuropas aus der Spätbronze- und frühen Eisenzeit, (9.– 6. Jahrhundert v. Chr. Geb.).* Munich, Bayerische Akademie der Wissenschaften, Philosophisch-Historische Klasse, Abhandlungen Neue Folge 116.

Kukoč, S. (2016) Pectoral lewelry and the Liburnians: reflections of the myth about sun's journey in the Liburnian culture. *Archaeologia Adriatica* 10(1), 7–101.

Laffineur, R. and Hägg, R. eds (2001) *Potnia. Deities and religion in the Aegean Bronze Age. Proceedings of the 8th international Aegean Conference ... Göteborg University, 12–15 April 2000.* Aegaeum 22.

Lo Schiavo, F. (1970) Il gruppo liburnico–japodico: per una definizione nell'ambito della protostoria balcanica. *Atti della Accademia nazionale dei Lincei. Classe di scienze morali, storiche e filologiche. Memorie* series 8 14 (6), 363–523.

Lo Schiavo, F. (1984) La Daunia e l'Adriatico. In *La civiltà dei Dauni nel quadro del mondo italico. Atti del XIII Convegno di Studi Etruschi e Italici (Manfredonia, 21–27 Giugno 1980),* 213–247. Firenze, Olschki.

Lucentini, N. (2001) I traffici interadriatici. In G. Colonna and L. Franchi Dall'Orto (eds) *Eroi e Regine. Piceni popolo d'Europa. Catalogo della mostra,* 58–60. Rome, De Luca.

Marino, D. (2008) *Prima di Kroton. Dalle comunità protostoriche alla nascita della città.* Crotone, Xila.

Martelli, M. (2004) Riflessioni sul santuario di Francavilla Marittima. *Bollettino d'Arte* 127, 1–24.

Marzatico, F. (2011) Forme e idee in movimento, dal sole al 'Signore e Signora degli animali'. In F. Marzatico, R. Gebhard, and P. Gleirscher (eds) *Le grandi vie della civiltà. Catalogo della mostra,* 327–333. Trento, Castello del Buonconsiglio.

Matthäus, H. (1980) Mykenische Vogelbarken. Antithetische Tierprotomen in der Kunst des östlichen Mittelmeerraumes. *Archäologisches Korrespondenzblatt* 10, 319–330.

Matthäus, H. (1981) Κυκνοι δε ησαν το αρμα. Spätmykenische und urnenfelderzeitliche Vogelplastik. In L. Herbert (ed.) *Studien zur Bronzezeit. Festschrift für Wilhelm Albert v. Brunn,* Mainz am Rhein, von Zabern, 277–297.

Melandri, G. (2011) *L'età del ferro a Capua. Aspetti distintivi del contesto culturale e suo inquadramento nelle dinamiche di sviluppo dell'Italia protostorica.* Oxford, British Archaeological Report S2265.

von Merhart, G. (1969) *Hallstatt und Italien. Gesammelte Aufsätze zur Frühen Eisenzeit in Italien und Mitteleuropa.* Mainz/Bonn, Verlag des römisch-germanischen Zentralmuseums Mainz.

Naso, A. (2016) Dall'Italia alla Grecia, IX – VII sec. a.C. In L. Donnellan, V. Nizzo and G.-J. Burgers (eds) *Contexts of Early Colonization. Atti del Convegno 'Contextualizing Early Colonization. Archaeology, Sources, Chronology and Interpretative Models between Italy and the Mediterranean' Rome 2012,* vol. 1, 275–287. Rome, Papers of the Royal Netherlands Institute in Rome 64.

Naso, A. (2020) Frauen der Früheisenzeit. Weibliche Tracht und ethnische Identität auf der italienischen Halbinsel am Beispiel der Cinturoni. *Mitteilungen des Deutschen Archäologischen Instituts. Roemische Abteilung* 126, 13–37.

Nava, M.L. (1988) *Le stele della Daunia*. Milano, Electa.

Nava, M.L. and Salerno, A. eds (2007) *Ambre. Trasparenze dall'antico. Catalogo della mostra, Napoli, Museo Archeologico Nazionale, 26 marzo–10 settembre 2007*. Milano, Electa.

Negroni Catacchio, N. (2011) Amber in antiquity. In A. Vianello (ed.) *Exotica in the Prehistoric Mediterranean*, 58–60. Oxford, Oxbow Books.

Negroni Catacchio, N. ed. (2016) *Ornarsi per comunicare con gli uomini e con gli Dei. Gli oggetti di ornamento come status symbol, amuleti, richiesta di protezione. Ricerche e scavi. Atti del XII Incontro di Studi 'Preistoria e Protostoria in Etruria' (Valentano, Pitigliano, Manciano, 12–14 settembre 2014)*. Milano, Centro Studi di Preistoria e Archeologia.

Nizzo, V. (2007) Le produzioni in bronzo di area medio-italica e dauno-lucana. In M.G. Benedettini (ed.) *Il Museo delle Antichità Etrusche e Italiche. II. Dall'incontro con il mondo greco alla romanizzazione*, 327–359. Rome, Università la Sapienza.

Nizzo, V. (2008) I materiali cumani del Museo Nazionale Preistorico Etnografico «Luigi Pigorini». *Bullettino di Paletnologia Italiana* 97, 165–276.

Nizzo, V. (2015) *Archeologia e antropologia della morte: storia di un'idea: la semiologia e l'ideologia funeraria delle società di livello protostorico nella riflessione teorica tra antropologia e acheologia*. Bari, Edipuglia.

Nizzo, V. (2018) 'A morte 'o ssajeched'è?': strategie e contraddizioni dell'antropo–pòiesi al margine tra la vita e la morte. Una prospettiva archeologica. In V. Nizzo (ed.) *Archeologia e antropologia della morte: 3. Costruzione e decostruzione del sociale. Atti del 3° Incontro Internazionale di Studi 'Antropologia e archeologia a confronto' (Roma, 20–22 maggio 2015)*, vol. 3, 91–235. Rome, Editorial Service System.

Nizzo, V. ed. (2020a) *Gli Etruschi e il MANN. Catalogo della mostra (Napoli, Museo Archeologico Nazionale 2020)*. Milano, Electa.

Nizzo, V. (2020b) Il carrellino cultuale del MANN. In Nizzo 2020a, 328.

Nizzo, V. (2020c) Pendaglio pettorale. In Nizzo 2020a, 57.

Nizzo, V. (2020d) Calatia, Tomba 201. In Nizzo 2020a, 104–105.

Pacciarelli, M. (2002) Raffigurazione di miti e riti su manufatti metallici di Bisenzio e Vulci tra il 750 e il 650 a. C. In A. Carandini (ed.) *Archeologia del Mito, Emozione e ragione fra primitivi e moderni*, 301–332. Torino, Einaudi.

Papadopoulos, J. K. (2003) *La dea di Sibari e il santuario ritrovato. Studi sui rinvenimenti dal Timpone Motta di Francavilla Marittima, II.1. The archaic votive metal objects*. *Bollettino d'Arte* special volume.

Percossi Serenelli, E. ed. (1998) *Museo Archeologico Nazionale delle Marche, Sezione Protostorica. I Piceni*. Falconara, Errebi.

Peroni, R. (1976) La «koiné» adriatica e il suo processo di formazione. In *Jadranska Obala u Protohistoriji Kulturni i etnicki problemi. Simpozij Odrzan o Dubrovniku 19–23 ottobre 1972*, 95–116. Zagreb, Liber.

Pietropaolo, L. ed. (2002) *Sformate immagini di bronzo. Il carrello di Lucera tra VIII e VII sec. a.C.*, Foggia. Grenzi.

Preložnik, A. (2021) Japodski i Liburnski antropomorfni privjesci/Iapodian and Liburnian anthropomorphic pendants. *Archaeologia Adriatica* 15, 201–239.

Rebay-Salisbury, K. (2016) *The Human Body in Early Iron Age Central Europe Burial Practices and Images of the Hallstatt World*. London/New York, Routledge.

Richardson, E. (1984) The lady at the fountain. In *Studi di antichità in onore di Guglielmo Maetzke*, 447–454. Rome, Bretschneider.

Rossi, F. (2005) *La dea sconosciuta e la barca solare. Una placchetta votiva del santuario protostorico di Breno in Valle Camonica*. Milano, ET Edizioni.

Spadea, R. (1997) Santuari di Hera a Crotone. In J. de La Genière (ed.) *Héra. Images, espaces, cultes. Actes du Colloque International du Centre de Recherches Archéologiques de l'Université de Lille III et de l'Association P.R.A.C. Lille, 29–30 novembre 1993*, 235–259. Naples, Publications du Centre Jean Bérard.

Trigger, B. G. (2007) *A History of Archaeological Thought*, 2nd ed. Cambridge, Cambridge University Press.

Wirth, S. (2006) Vogel-Sonnen-Barke. In H. Beck, D. Geuenich and H. Steuer (eds) *Reallexikon der Germanischen Altertumskunde*, 552–563. Berlin/New York, de Gruyter.

Chapter 7

Responsibilities, obedience and righteousness: other-than-human creatures in the Hebrew Bible

Mari Joerstad

It is clear from such texts as Genesis 1 and Leviticus 18–26 that other-than-human creatures in the Hebrew Bible have divinely appointed responsibilities. The sun, moon and stars are appointed to rule the night and the day. The land must rest on the sabbath. This paper will consider how the ancient authors of the Hebrew Bible conceptualized divine responsibilities given to other-than-human creatures. I look first at texts in which creatures receive responsibilities, then at texts in which they fail to uphold them and finally at texts in which other-than-human creatures enable or enact righteousness. Together, these texts suggest that biblical authors saw no sharp distinction between human and other-than-human responsibilities. Further, every creature depends on every other creature to fulfil their obligations. When one creature fails, everyone suffers. The responsibility to right wrongs does not lie with humans alone or primarily. In the final set of texts, water is a particularly important creature in restoring the land to righteousness.

Introduction

To whom does God give responsibilities in the Hebrew Bible and what does it mean to receive a responsibility? And what happens if we ask these questions through the lens of animism?

In this chapter, I will look at obligation, obedience and righteousness as creation-wide responsibilities. I will look at texts in the Hebrew Bible that treat other-than-human creatures as active partners in upholding divine edicts, rather than as the background to or the tools of human relationships with God. I will argue that righteousness and the related concepts of obedience and disobedience are not, in the Hebrew Bible, human concerns only. Rather, when God enjoins Israel to be obedient,

Israel participates in a responsibility that extends beyond humans to include other beings.

I will begin from the assumption that Graham Harvey's description of animists as 'people who recognise that the world is full of persons, only some of whom are human, and that life is always lived in relationship with others' is an accurate description of ancient Israelites (Harvey 2005, xi).[1] Methodologically, animism provides a rationale for treating other-than-human beings as characters in the story. The examples I will give in this chapter may feel like a grab-bag. If thought of through modernist concepts of agency and morality, it is not clear that they belong together. What I hope to accomplish by putting them side by side is to point the way to a reframing of how we understand creaturely responsibility. At the heart of this is the idea that creaturely responsibility is first and foremost about sustaining and perpetuating life. This means that concepts like will and guilt are insufficient. Instead, my focus will be on communal health and the various ways in which all creatures contribute to that health, with community here being understood as encompassing all creatures: plant, animal, human, mineral and so on.

The chapter is divided into three main sections. First, I will look at texts in which other-than-human creatures receive responsibilities from God. Second, I will look at texts in which they are either unable or unwilling to uphold those responsibilities. Finally, I will consider texts in which other-than-human creatures contribute to and make possible righteousness.

Receiving responsibilities

It is clear from such texts as Genesis 1 and Leviticus 18–26 that other-than-human creatures in the Hebrew Bible have divinely appointed responsibilities. In Genesis 1, the sun and the moon are charged with making a distinction (הַבְדִּיל) between light and dark, being signs (אֹתֹת) for seasons, giving light (הָאִיר) to the earth, and ruling (מָשַׁל) the day and the night (Genesis 1:14–18). Of these, two tasks resemble human responsibilities – to make a distinction and to rule – but the text does not distinguish between what we might think of as personal functions (see Westermann 1984, 127) and things that the sun and the moon do just by being the sun and the moon.

In Leviticus, the land is charged with the responsibility of keeping sabbath (Morgan 2009). We learn of this responsibility indirectly, through edicts that charge Israel with the responsibility to support and not hinder the land's sabbaths: 'When you enter the land which I am giving you, the land is to rest – a sabbath to YHWH' (Leviticus 25:2). If the land cannot keep sabbath because Israel obstructs it, the land will send its people into exile: 'Then the land will enjoy its sabbaths, all the days it lies desolate, and you are in the land of your enemies. Then the land will pay off its sabbaths. All the days it lies desolate it will rest, [the rest] it did not rest during your sabbaths when you rested[2] upon it' (Leviticus 26:34–35). The land's responsibility to observe sabbath is not a roundabout way of speaking of human sabbaths. If humans

But the issue is to stop work and only humans work the land.

get in the way of the land's sabbath, the land must find a way to observe it anyway, by ejecting its humans.

I begin with these examples of responsibilities because they are the ones that sound the most incongruent to modern, Western ears. As such, they are helpful for getting us into the frame of mind that all creatures have responsibilities. The most common responsibility in the Hebrew Bible, however, is one that is shared by the earth, the seas, plants, animals and humans, that is, to reproduce and make life.

The language differs depending on the creature in question. When speaking of plants, the language of seeds and fruit dominates: 'plants sowing seeds and fruit trees making fruit according to its kind, which has its seed in it' (Genesis 1:11). When speaking to the sea and the earth, the focus is not on perpetuating one's own species, but bringing forth animals, birds and fish: 'Let the waters swarm with living, swarming things' (Genesis 1:20). For fish, birds and humans, we have the familiar command 'to be fruitful and multiply' (Genesis 1:22, 28). The overall point in each example is the same: all creatures have a responsibility to perpetuate life. When we now move to texts in which other-than-human nature fails in some way at its responsibilities, this is the responsibility that is usually in view.

Failing to fulfil responsibilities

Texts that describe other-than-human creatures receiving edicts from God are few, but texts in which other-than-human creatures either cannot or will not fulfil their obligations are more numerous. This is primarily because many texts in the Hebrew Bible treat human failures and the failures of human and other-than-human creatures are intimately related. The inability or unwillingness of any creature to be and do what they are tasked with affects all other creatures. When humans fail to fulfil their obligations to God, they often make it impossible for other creatures to do so as well.[3] I will look at three ways in which writers of the Bible describe other-than-human creatures' failure to fulfil obligation – sickness, mourning and sin.

Sickness

Biblical authors sometime interpret a creature's inability to fulfil their obligations as illness. An example is the healing of the waters found in 2 Kings 2:19-22:

> The people of the city spoke to Elisha: notice, the setting of the city is good, as my lord can see, but the waters are bad and the land is bereaved. He said: Get me a new vessel and put salt in it ... He went out to the spring of the water and he threw salt into it. He said: thus says YHWH: I have healed these waters. No longer will death and bereavement come from there.

There are several things to note: First, the waters themselves are described as bad, רָעִים, which can denote anything from something of low quality to something evil. Second, the waters spread sickness: death and bereavement come from them. Bereavement here does not refer to human bereavement only. The land as a whole is bereaved. Third, the process of fixing the waters is described as healing. It is the same word used for the healing of human wounds, be it through prophetic intercession or by a physician.

It is possible to argue that words for sickness and healing have different meanings when applied to humans and to non-humans. For example, in Ezekiel 47, we have another example of waters healed: the river that comes out from the temple heals the stagnant waters. It is clear that healing here means desalination, because the marshes and swamps are not healed, but 'left for salt' (לְמֶלַח נִתְּנוּ) (47:11).

However, in both the Kings and Ezekiel texts, the purpose of healing is life for the wider community – both the swarming things that live in water and the plants and animals that depend on water. In Kings, the land will no longer be bereaved. In Ezekiel, the river brings life: 'Wherever the rivers go, all living things that swarm will live, and fish will be very plentiful. For these waters will go there and they will be healed and live, wherever the river goes' (Ezekiel 47:9). In other words, sick waters make lands sick, and healed waters heals the whole land community. The central concern of each text is not the distinction between salt and fresh water, but how the communal ability to sustain and pass on life requires a sick creature – waters – to regain health so that it can house and support other life.

Deuteronomy 29:21 also uses the language of illness to speak of land: 'The next generation...will see the wounds of this land and the diseases (תַּחֲלֻאֶיהָ) with which YHWH has made the land sick.' The context is the covenant oath between God and Israel in Deuteronomy. If Israel abandons the covenant, God will make the land sick, so sick it cannot support plants: 'brimstone and salt burning all its soil, nothing sowed and nothing sprouting, no vegetation growing in it' (Deut. 29:22). It is another clear example of failure to sustain life, but unlike the example from Kings, the reason for the illness is human action, described metaphorically as a poisonous plant: 'a root fruiting poison and wormwood' (Deut. 29:18). Like in Leviticus, human disobedience here frustrates the life of the land.

Grief

The language of grief is concentrated in the prophets and, unlike sickness, the grief of other-than-human nature is almost always a result of human activity interfering in their life (on the motif of the land mourning, see Hayes 2002). A representative example is Jeremiah 12:11: 'They have turned it into a desolation. It mourns to me, desolate. The whole earth is made desolate, but no one takes it to heart'.

Like texts that describe sickness, mourning is associated with a difficulty in maintaining plant, animal and human life. For example, Hosea 4:3 catalogues the devastation that has come upon the land because of human bloodshed: 'Therefore the earth mourns and all its inhabitants languish, with the animals of the field, the birds of the heavens, and the fish of the sea, they die'.

These texts do not suggest that the earth, the fish, the birds or the animals have done anything wrong. But they do suggest that they are frustrated in their proper living. A desolate land is a kind of negative image of Genesis 1, a creational undoing (see, for example, van Ruiten 2005). That which is made to sprout, seed, teem, fly, creep, eat and procreate is absent in desolate landscapes.

The synonyms for שְׁמָמָה, desolation, illustrates this. The most common parallel expressions are ones that describe the absence of inhabitants, like מֵאֵין יוֹשֵׁב (without inhabitants, see Isaiah 6:11, see also Jeremiah 6:8; 9:10(and מֵאֵין אָדָם (without humans, Jeremiah 34:22; 44:6; 49:2, 33; 50:13; Ezekiel 6:14; 12:20; 14:15). Not just human inhabitants, but animals and plants as well, though a few wild animals like jackals (תַּנִּים), are associated with the term. To modern readers, an empty land does not necessarily sound like a frustrated land. But in the Hebrew Bible the ideal land is one teeming with inhabitants. For example, Ezekiel 36:12 likens inhabitants to the land's children (Greenberg 1997, 72).

To be devastated is sometimes necessary, as we see in Leviticus 26, in which the land spews out its inhabitants in order to pay back its missed sabbaths ('Then the land will enjoy its sabbaths, all the days it lies desolate and you are in the land of your enemies' [Leviticus 26:34]). But as we have already seen, this desolation, like the other prophetic examples of land in mourning, is caused by human failures to uphold the covenant. Desolation as such is never desirable. It is sometimes necessary when different obligations come into conflict with each other. In the case of Leviticus, human refusal to observe sabbath makes the land unable to observe sabbath. To address this, the land throws out its inhabitants, with the result that the land is in a less than ideal state of supporting life. The obligation to keep sabbath and the obligation to sustain life are here in conflict, because part of the life the land sustains – human life – is disrupting the communal ability to meet covenant obligations.

Sin and abomination
In the cases of sickness and mourning, failures to fulfil obligations are either blamed on no-one or on humans. It is rare that the language of sin is applied to other-than-human creatures.

The exception is Ezekiel. While Ezekiel certainly speaks of human sin, the oracles are often concerned with the land itself.[4] For example, in Ezekiel 14, God explains to Ezekiel what God does to a land that sins: 'Mortal, when a land sins against me by acting unfaithfully ... I stretch out my hand against it and I break from it [the] staff of bread and I send into it famine and I cut from it human and animal ...' (Ezekiel 14:12).

These consequences are similar to those seen in Jeremiah and Isaiah, though they are there described as devastation and mourning. It is tempting to think that 'land' here is just a stand-in for humans, but there are many other examples in Ezekiel.

For example, in Ezekiel 6, the prophet prophecies directly to the land:

> The word of YHWH came to me, saying: Mortal, set your face against the mountains of Israel and prophecy against them. You are to say: Mountains of Israel, hear the word of the Lord YHWH. Thus says the Lord YHWH to the mountains and to the hills and to the ravines and to the valleys: Look! I am bringing against you a sword, and I will destroy your high places. Your altars will be desolate and your incense altars will be broken and I will make your slain fall before your idols. And I will set the corpses of the children of Israel before your idols, and I will scatter your bones round about your altars. In all your dwelling places, cities will be waste, and the high places desolate, so that your altars will be waste and desolate, your idols broken and destroyed, your incense altars hewn, and your work wiped out. The slain will fall in your midst, and you will know that I am YHWH. (Ezekiel 6:1–7)

Ezekiel 7 tells us why God is punishing the land – it contains abominations: 'Thus says the Lord YHWH to the soil of Israel: ... Now the end is upon you, and I will let loose my anger against you, and I will judge you according to your ways, and I will repay you for all your abominations' (Ezekiel 7:1, 3). Outside Ezekiel, the books most interested in abominations are Leviticus and Deuteronomy.[5] In these books, certain human actions are considered abominations (תּוֹעֵבָה) and can make the land unclean (תְּטָמָא). In Jeremiah 2:7, human action transforms the land itself into an abomination. But Ezekiel is unique in accusing the land of abominable practices.

Note that Ezekiel is not interpreting a different set of conditions than Jeremiah and Isaiah. Drought, absence of humans and animals, failure of crops, and war – these are the same events that Isaiah and Jeremiah interpret at grief. But Ezekiel frames them in a different light, by holding the land responsible in a way that Isaiah and Jeremiah do not.

Taken together

Taken together, sickness, mourning and sin suggest a view of responsibility that goes beyond guilt. You can be responsible for something without necessarily being guilty when it does not happen and yet you suffer the consequences. Failure to uphold life has more-or-less the same consequences, whether it results from disobedience, the obstruction of other creatures or unexplained illness.

Having been given divine responsibilities, other-than-human creatures are held accountable when they fail to uphold them, regardless of the reason. Particularly interesting is the view in Ezekiel, that land can sin. It suggests a broad similarity between human moral and religious responsibilities and those of other-than-human creatures. Other creatures have the capability of being disobedient. What we might think of as instinct, the biblical authors think of more as obedient action, and, when those instinct are frustrated, as disobedience, or at least as hindered obedience.

Righteousness

If land can sin, can it also be described as righteous? Two prophetic texts suggest that yes, the other-than-human world provides or contributes to righteousness. The first is Isaiah 45:8:

Drip, O heavens, from above, and let the clouds stream righteousness. Let the earth open so that salvation may bear fruit, and let it make righteousness sprout together. I, YHWH, have created it.

Joel also associates rain and righteousness:

Do not be afraid, O soil, be glad and rejoice. For the YHWH has done great things. Do not be afraid, O animals of [the] field for the pastures of the wilderness will be green, for the tree will carry its fruit and the fig and the vine will give their strength. O children of Zion, rejoice and be glad in YHWH your God, for he has given you the early rain for righteousness, and he has brought down on you rain, early rain and later rain, like before. (Joel 2:21–23)

A final text, Zechariah 8:12, assigns to other-than-human nature the ability to cultivate *shalom*, wellbeing or peace:

For there will be a sowing of wellbeing (זֶרַע הַשָּׁלוֹם). The vine will give its fruit and the earth will give its produce, and the heavens will give its dew. And I will cause the remnant of this people to inherit all these things. (Zechariah 8:12)

Just as drought and aridity is associated with sickness, mourning, and sin, so righteousness and peace are associated with rain and with abundant growth. This makes sense on an intuitive level – fruitful landscapes sound nicer than ones devastated by drought – but there is more to these associations than that.

We have seen that human action can impede the ability of other creatures to fulfil their obligations. But here we see that humans are dependent on other creatures to return to righteousness. If one of the most important responsibilities of all creatures is to sustain and perpetuate life, that makes sense. Humans cannot, by independent action, make it rain or make fruit trees produce fruit. Human disobedience can lead to desolate landscapes, but human obedience is not enough to restore the land to health. The most important creature in this regard is water, which enables other creatures – plants, animals and humans – to flourish. The biblical authors do not describe the return of life to land passively, as the automatic or mechanical result of rain, but as the active participation of a whole host of creatures, beginning with rain, but extending to fruit trees and vines, clouds, soil, animals and humans.

Conclusion

Divine responsibilities are understood in a relational fashion in the Hebrew Bible, and responsibility is never individual. Creatures need each other in order to fulfil obligations and are also held responsible for each other's failures. This is in large part because obligations are not tests of obedience; they are not random rules. Divine obligations set out what is required of each creature in order for the whole community to thrive.

I have used Genesis 1 as a reference point several times. There's nothing special about Genesis 1. I do not mean to say that the writers of other biblical texts necessarily had Genesis 1 in mind. But Genesis 1 is one of the texts that comes closest to an explanation of biblical worldviews, a text which describes the ideal life of each creature. It provides a reason to put together texts that we might otherwise think of as belonging to different conceptual spheres.

Returning to the quote from Graham Harvey with which I started, that animists are 'people who recognise that the world is full of persons, only some of whom are human, and that life is always lived in relationship with others' (Harvey 2005, xi), what can we now say? First, divine edicts, whether they are aimed at human or other-than-human creatures, do not simply fall into the category of morality or spirituality. Obligation in the Hebrew Bible is practical, ecological and relational. That is not to say that it is not also moral and spiritual. But even the moral or spiritual dimensions are always communal and relational. No one enacts obedience or disobedience on their own, nor is anyone shielded from the actions of others. The point is not some abstract internal state of holiness but the whole community's ability to flourish and live well together.

Second, biblical authors make no clear categorical separation between human responsibilities and other-than-human responsibilities. We do not see something akin to the modern distinction between instinct and agency. The Hebrew Bible focuses primarily on human actions, because it is a human book, but all creatures are considered responsible for their own life and their contribution to the life of the world. When the sun rises and sets each day, biblical authors see obedience (see Psalm 19). When a fruit tree does not bear fruit, biblical authors assume the fruit tree is either sick, kept from fruitfulness by the disobedience of others or itself disobedient. When fruit trees do bear fruit, biblical authors interpret this as generosity (Zechariah 8:12).

Third, when biblical authors try to evaluate whether Israel is fulfiling its obligations, they often look to the state of the land. Their modes of evaluation, however, are not simplistic. It is a bit of a truism in biblical studies that the land of Israel serves as a thermometer of Israel's faithfulness to their covenant with YHWH, much like the painting in *The Picture of Dorian Gray* (Wilde 2020 [1890]). This assigns a subordinate and mechanical role to the land, rather than seeing the land and humans as mutually dependent on each other. But the relationship between human conduct and the state of the land is neither automatic nor one-way. It would be equally true to say that the state of human society can reflect the faithfulness of the land – this is what Ezekiel suggests. The land is neither a mechanical nor random indicator of human conduct. Instead, humans, soils, plants and animals all depend on each other to fulfil covenant obligations. If one creature cannot or will not fulfil their role, all others suffer. The Hebrew Bible spends most time on human obligations, but human obligations are not more or less important than those of other creatures.

This is not to 'naturalize' the cause and effect of how righteousness and communal health relate to each other. The relationship between conduct and the health of the land community is not described in an analogous way to how we think today of, for example, the anthropogenic origins of climate change. God is often an active participant in managing the relationship. There is a deep sense of interdependence in the Hebrew Bible, but that interdependence does not always match how modern-day ecology thinks of interdependence.

There is not space here to do a thorough comparison with how the bible described human obligation, obedience, and disobedience, but I think that would be useful. In particular, looking at the legal corpus in the Torah through this lens might provide new insights into the role of law in the Bible. I am from a Protestant tradition and we struggle with law (to put it mildly). Attention to the role of other-than-human creatures may help us get passed the association of law with guilt and will, and obedience as an internal state. It might instead help us read law as instructions in communal living, ways of marking and shaping how humans interact with each other, but also with other creatures: farm animals, gazelles, soil, fruit trees and cedars, clouds and rivers. If responsibility is not primarily about individual goodness, law looks very different. But that discussion is for another time.

Notes

1 For a defence of this assumption, see Joerstad (2019).
2 I have translated יָשַׁב here as 'rested', in order to reproduce in English the wordplay between the root שבת and בְּשִׁבְתְּכֶם, the infinitive construct of יָשַׁב.
3 For more on the implications of the interdependence of humans and other creatures, see Fretheim (2005, 269–284).
4 This aspect of Ezekiel has faced critique in eco-hermeneutics. See Stevenson (2001), Carley (2001) and Habel (2004).
5 For details on how Ezekiel's presentation of land builds on Leviticus, see Kelle (2009).

References

Carley, K. (2001) Ezekiel's formula of desolation: harsh justice for the land/earth. In N.C. Habel (ed.) *The Earth Story in Psalms and Prophets,* 143–157. Sheffield, Sheffield Academic.

Fretheim, T.E. (2005) *God and the World in the Old Testament: a relational theology of creation.* Nashville TN, Abingdon.

Greenberg, M. (1997) *Ezekiel 21-37: a new translation with introduction and commentary.* New York, Doubleday.

Habel, N.C. (2004) The silence of the lands: the ecojustice implications of Ezekiel's judgement oracles. In Habel, N.C. *Ezekiel's Hierarchical World: wrestling with a tiered reality,* 127–140. Atlanta GA, Society of Biblical Literature.

Harvey, G. (2005) *Animism: respecting the living world.* London, Hurst.

Hayes, K.M. (2002) *The Earth Mourns: prophetic metaphor and oral aesthetic.* Atlanta GA, Society of Biblical Literature.

Joerstad, M. (2019) *The Hebrew Bible and Environmental Ethics: humans, nonhumans, and the living landscape.* Cambridge, Cambridge University Press.

Kelle, B.E. (2009) Dealing with the trauma of defeat: the rhetoric of the devastation and rejuvenation of nature in Ezekiel. *Journal of Biblical Literature* 128, 469–490.

Morgan, J. (2009) Transgressing, puking, covenanting: the character of land in Leviticus. *Theology* 112, 172–180.

van Ruiten, J. (2005) Back to chaos: the relationship between Jeremiah 4:23–26 and Genesis 1. In G.H. Van Kooten (ed.) *The Creation of Heaven and Earth: Re-Interpretations of Genesis 1 in the Context of Judaism, Ancient Philosophy, Christianity, and Modern Physics*, 21–30. Leiden: Brill Themes in Biblical Narrative 8.

Stevenson, K.R. (2001) If Earth could speak: the case of the mountains against YHWH in Ezekiel 6:35–36. In Habel, N.C. (ed.). *The Earth Story in Psalms and Prophets*, 158–171. Sheffield, Sheffield Academic.

Westermann, C. (1984) *Genesis 1-11: a commentary.* Minneapolis MN, Augsburg.

Wilde, O. (2020) [1890] *The Picture of Dorian Gray: authoritative texts, backgrounds, reviews and reactions, criticism* (ed. D.L. Lawler). New York, W.W. Norton & Company.